Fein, Leonard J
  The ecology of the public schools; an inquiry into community control, by Leonard J. Fein.   New York, Pegasus ₍c1971₎

  vii, 170 p.   illus.   21 cm.   (Pegasus series on decentralization and the urban crisis, 2)

  Includes bibliographical references.

  1. Community and school.   2. Segregation in education—United States.   3. Negroes—Education.   I. Title.

LC215.F4   370.19'344   70-128661
                                                                                    MARC

Library of Congress   . 72₍72₎

THE ECOLOGY OF

THE PUBLIC SCHOOLS

THE ECOLOGY OF

THE PUBLIC SCHOOLS

AN INQUIRY INTO COMMUNITY CONTROL

BY LEONARD J. FEIN

PEGASUS · NEW YORK

A DIVISION OF THE BOBBS-MERRILL COMPANY, INC., PUBLISHERS

This is the second volume in the "Pegasus Series on Decentralization and the Urban Crisis," of which Alan Altshuler is General Editor.

The first volume in the Series is *Community Control: The Black Demand for Participation in Large American Cities* by Alan Altshuler.

The author is grateful for permission to reprint Figures 1, 2, 3, and 4: copyright by the President and Fellows of Harvard College.

CONTENTS

PREFACE

THE "BEST" relationship between communities and their schools has been a matter of substantial concern in American educational theory and practice since public schools were created. Until recently, the issue was debated primarily at the local level, with each of the thousands of school districts seeking its own truth. Now, however, the issue has taken on a major national dimension, and, as a result, has become far more visible than it traditionally had been.

As is the wont in such matters, public attention has focused primarily on the most voluble participants in the debate. While passion is surely appropriate in matters of great consequence, the danger is always that what begins as an argument passionately presented will end as a passion passionately argued. It has seemed to me that there are very serious issues at stake in the debate over community control of the schools, issues which touch those of us whose educational destinies do not seem, in the first instance, to be at stake, scarcely less than they touch the chief protagonists. This book seeks to state those issues in their most general context, and, thereby, to insure that the debate will not be left solely to those who appear to have the most immediate interest in their resolution.

I have benefited greatly from the advice and criticism of my colleague and friend, Alan Altshuler, and from my brother and friend, Rashi Fein; I owe special thanks also to John Mong, who persuaded me to undertake the effort. I hereby absolve these good gentlemen from responsibility for the deficiencies of the product. My wife, Zelda, would not accept such absolution. That is her special virtue, and that is why this book is for her.

L. J. F.

INTRODUCTION

IN THE SUMMER of 1967, the Chicago Board of Education published the Redmond Report, *Increasing Desegregation of Facilities, Students, and Vocational Education Programs*. The Report called for a massive program of bussing black children into white neighborhoods to guarantee integrated education for Chicago. Had such a report been issued ten years earlier, or even two years earlier, it would doubtless have been widely hailed as a landmark document, a historically progressive commitment on the part of a public agency.

In the fall of 1968, the State Board of Education in Massachusetts issued its annual report on racial imbalance in the public schools. The report showed that 71.7% of the black students of Boston attended schools that were, under the definition of the law, racially imbalanced. Three years earlier, when the annual report showed a lower proportion of Negro students attending racially imbalanced schools, its publication was attended by a torrent of condemnation.

Save for brief flurries of comment by liberal newspapers, both the Redmond Report and the Report on Racial Imbalance in the Schools were greeted by a yawn, most particularly by the very communities whose educational conditions they sought to affect. The attention of many Negro leaders, by late 1967, had turned quite decisively away from issues of integration, not only in New York City, where new issues were most dramatically raised, but in many other cities around the country.

Negro demands for control of the schools their children attend have moved from relative obscurity to crippling confrontation with astonishing speed, eclipsing and sometimes

1

emasculating continuing efforts at integration. No wonder,
then, that white liberals are substantially bewildered; fighting
valiantly on the battlefields of integration, they now discover
the most articulate of their presumed beneficiaries engaged
in a very different war.

Nor is liberal zeal the only casualty of the move towards
community control of the schools. If it were, we would
hardly witness so intense, so acrimonious a debate as now we
do. More is at stake, evidently, than the temporary discomfort of a relatively small group. Either explicitly, in the
rhetoric of those who challenge the established order, or
implicitly, in the projected consequences of community control, traditional theories of public education, common understandings of the good society, and accepted conventions
regarding the distribution of public power in America, are
all called into question. Thus it is not surprising to find this
emergent issue both supported and resisted hyperbolically.

Yet hyperbole, however useful it may be as rhetoric, is
inadequate as analysis. Although substantial numbers of
people have come to endorse community control with passion
and to see their destinies wrapped up in its success, it
cannot be left solely to the protagonists to argue it out, for
its implications are profound. Moreover, precisely because
the movement towards community control has split the
liberal community, and thereby threatened the traditional
civil rights alliance in this country in the aftermath of its
most impressive victories, the problems it raises and the
opportunities it affords must be presented fully. That is what
this book is about, although the debate is still too urgent and
too unfolding, the evidence too fragmentary and conflicting,
to permit a conclusive statement. What is intended, instead,
is some clarification, some assertion of boundaries for the
continuing debate, and, perhaps, an agenda for further discussion.

Writing in defense of the community control position,
Charles Hamilton asks rhetorically, "Who can predict what
the 'tests' will show when we begin to expose black children

to these kinds of innovations?"[1] The answer he implies is that men of good will can readily predict, and the prediction is that black children will do much better. The real answer, however, is that no one can confidently predict what the results might be. There is, as yet, no basis for such prediction, for there are far too few cases for study and there has been far too imprecise an evaluation of even these few cases. We are required, instead, to argue from theory and from informed inference. Yet we are required to argue, for there is no denying, not any more, that the item is on the public agenda, and very near the top. Many might have wished it otherwise, might have wished that the traditional alliance had persisted in its efforts to break through the debilitating walls of segregation. Perhaps, in the unlikely event that those who continue to fight that battle suddenly score some victories, community control will recede as an important policy question. But the record of the seventeen years since the Supreme Court initiated desegregation of America's public schools hardly gives rise to optimism that major victories are just around the corner, nor does the apparent confusion of the Nixon administration regarding integration provide much cause for hope. In the meantime, even those who view the doctrine of community control with misgiving, or worse, may yet take some comfort from the fact that this is quite likely the first time in American history that Negroes themselves have exercised agenda-making power for the society at large. It is testament to how far we have come, in recent years, as a society, and how far black people have come, as a group, that they can so directly affect the nation's agenda. And yet, between the agenda and the decision comes the debate; that is what these pages are about.

My first, and preliminary, concern is to trace some of the threads which have led to a rejection of the goal of integrated education. I neither intend nor have the capacity to tell the whole of this truth, for it is a truth compounded of massive detail. I turn, then, to what I perceive to be the main theoretical underpinnings of the new departure, and examine community control as it bears upon first, understandings of society; second, understandings of democratic politics; and third, issues in educational theory. In the course of exploring these theoretical questions, I am less concerned with analysis of the public statements of the several protagonists, more with the merits and limits of the case, as best I have been able to assess them. Finally, I raise several issues of general public policy which seem to me critical in forming a judgment on the issue.

CHAPTER ONE

BACKGROUND TO CONTROVERSY

The Failure of Integration

IN DOZENS, if not hundreds, of American cities the struggle to desegregate public education continues. Here and there, one encounters striking success and, in some places, cause for hope. But the fact remains that seventeen years after the Supreme Court initiated the process, the overwhelming majority of black students in America are still attending schools that are largely segregated. In 1969, over 87 per cent of all Negro public school students were enrolled in schools in which over 50 per cent of the students body was black, and almost 65 per cent were in schools that were 95 per cent (or more) black.[1] Moreover, in city after city, segregation increased rather than declined during the 1960's.

No one can know how different the debate over education might now be had integration happened in America in the 1960's. There is at least some reason to suppose that the performance of Negro students would have improved.[2] But integration did not happen. Instead of happening, it was debated. And the debate, though it did not lead to significant action, was not without effect. On the contrary, the issues raised in the debate, in quite unanticipated ways, gave rise to the current movement towards community control.

As it became clear that integration would not easily be accepted, it seemed reasonable to its supporters to increase their efforts. Insofar as those efforts were directed at the conscience of white America—and that was, aside from the courts, their main target—they took the form of describing the effects of continuing segregation as sordidly as possible. The evidence, whether statistical or anecdotal, was not hard to come by, and it was presented forcefully and endlessly. Few white Americans could have remained unaware of the plight of Negro schoolchildren.

Whether another strategy, based on a more selective application of political power, might have worked, is now a moot question.[3] That the appeal to conscience did not work especially well is, however, clear. For though sympathy for the victim may have grown over the period between 1954 and 1966, the sympathy was based on a recognition of how badly off Negro students were. And the worse the depiction of their conditions, the more reluctant white parents could be expected to feel about involving themselves and their own children in the remedy.

In effect, the liberal community, both black and white, was caught up in a wrenching dilemma. The only way, it appeared, to move a sluggish nation towards massive amelioration of the Negro condition was to show how terrifyingly debilitating were the effects of discrimination and bigotry. The more lurid the detail, the more guilt it would evoke, and the more guilt, the more readiness to act. Yet the same lurid detail that did, in the event, prompt large-scale federal programs, also reinforced white convictions that Negroes were undesirable objects of interaction.

In retrospect, it is somewhat difficult to understand why this was not foreseen. Liberals insisted on broadcasting the very serious consequences of discrimination, including, in particular, the social and personal disorganization of Negro lives. All problematic aspects of Negro behavior—say, for example, crime—were explained away as the results of white oppression. Many whites were prepared to accept these explanations, and belief in theories of genetic inferiority were widely discredited. But understanding why a person is an illiterate, or a rascal, or even a criminal, may at best evoke a certain sympathy—even a readiness to pay higher taxes in order to repair the unhappy conditions which made the person that way—it does not, nor can it be expected to, promote a desire for increased interaction, and most assuredly not for residential integration which, given a commitment to neighborhood schools, is "required" if school integration is to be achieved. On the contrary, insofar as personal contact is concerned, it serves instead to reinforce the desire to avoid black people, by reinforcing already negative stereotypes.

In itself, this may not be a bad strategy. If carefully pursued, it might, for example, have the following results: whites, alerted to the evils of discrimination but anxious to avoid interaction with Negroes, increasingly support government programs designed to deal with the disabilities of blacks. As government programs succeed in relieving the disabilities, and Negro behavior seems less threatening, negative stereotypes begin to weaken. (This is quite a lengthy process, since there is, typically, a substantial lag between the shift in reality and the shift in perception.) As stereotypes weaken, integration becomes possible.

But: if integration is itself necessary in order to deal with the alleged inadequacies of blacks—if integration is a necessary means, and not only a desired end—as, in fact, specialists in education in particular have asserted, then we are in very serious trouble. For the arguments which might be used to persuade people to support government programs are the same arguments that people use to defend their hostility to integration.

Hence the very public and very prolonged debate over integration has not been entirely beneficent. It did not lead to integration itself, and, insofar as it changed white attitudes, it may well have changed them in rather negative ways.

Nor have whites been the only audience to the debate. Negroes have been parties of somewhat greater interest, and it is not at all clear, despite the continuing support which Negroes give to integrated education,[4] that they have been encouraged by the arguments of integrationists. Clearly, if such matters were taken into account at all, those who mounted the hustings for integration imagined that Negroes would support them, be grateful for their efforts, and take heart from the fact that some white Americans were championing the Negro cause. Once again, if integration actually had taken place, that might well have been the end of it. But the repeated pronouncements over the years, targeted towards the white conscience, stressing incessantly how unacceptable were the conditions of black education yet not producing much in the way of action, served instead to generate outraged impatience among black parents. It was one thing to know that your own children were having some difficulty in school, or perhaps even that the schools serving the children of your community were inadequate. It was quite another thing to be informed that the situation was absolutely intolerable, that nothing less than "educational genocide" was being inflicted on your children, and that the fundamental cause was a system at best impassive, at worst, maliciously racist.

Since this information was produced at about the same time that the federal government was busily promoting community organization, stimulating the growth of black protest movements and providing them with significant financial resources, it was natural for education to become a major target of protest. Further, this was a time when education was widely seen as *the* vehicle of social and economic mobility, *the* place to break the cycle of poverty.

More important still, persistent demands for integration were based on a rationale which was implicitly insulting to Negroes in a way that the simpler struggle for desegregation had not been. The insult was by no means obvious, and might, perhaps, have passed unnoticed had the debate been less protracted. But in the end, it became quite clear. So long as it was possible to maintain that the central reason for the poor performance of black children in the schools was embedded in the inadequacy of the schools themselves—in the age of the buildings, or the youth of the teachers, or even in the failure of school boards to provide black schools with equal resources—the argument was simple. The problem was clear, and the villain was clear. But the move towards integration could not be based solely on the perceived inadequacies of black schools. For if such inadequacies were the only source of the problem, then the solution need not have pointed to integration. Massive compensatory programs, seeking at a minimum to bring the facilities and staff of predominantly black schools up to white standards, or even, maximally, going beyond those standards in order to compensate for the special problems of black neighborhoods, would have been quite sufficient. Such programs would likely have cost more than white society was willing to pay, but it would have been less volatile politically than integration.

Emphasis on integration rather than compensation proceeded from the assumption that more than inadequate facilities and incompetent teachers lay at the roots of Negro failure. That assumption was massively confirmed—or appeared to be—by the Coleman Report,* which demonstrated that differences in plant and personnel were neither so great as had been supposed nor so significant in their educational impact as had been assumed. The achievement of school children, the Report argued, depends centrally on who their classmates are.

It was not surprising that some black leaders read the Report to say that "when you mix Negroes with Negroes, you get stupidity." For if the problem of black schools is not that they are institutionally inadequate, then it must lie in their very blackness. The argument of the Coleman Report was actually far more subtle, and far more complex. But subtleties and complexities have a way of getting lost on public platforms. The Report seemed to say that there was a

* See note 2.

mysterious disability at work in black schools, and that was
neither an easy nor a pleasant fact to come to grips with.
Inevitably, other interpretations were proposed; thus, one
group of black parents in Detroit could say:

> We charge that the basic reason for the failure to edu-
> cate inner city children stems from the schools' deliber-
> ate and systematic destruction of the Afro-American
> child's self-image and racial pride. Numerous aspects
> of Board policy contribute to this systematic destruc-
> tion of our children's belief in themselves. The policy of
> providing superior 'open schools' in the white outlying
> areas to which small numbers of privileged inner city
> children may be permitted to go and the policy of bus-
> sing Black children to 'white schools,' for example,
> express the underlying philosophy that quality education
> cannot be provided in inner city schools because if you
> mix Black with Black you can only get stupidity,
> whereas if you mix Black with white you must get some-
> thing superior to anything all-Black and somewhat in-
> ferior to anything all-white.[5]

The white liberal position failed to meet this criticism. In
the important decision in Hobson v. Hansen, Federal Judge
Skelly Wright held that "Racially and socially homogeneous
schools damage the minds and spirit of all children who
attend them—the Negro, the white, the poor, and the affluent
—and block the attainment of the broader goals of democratic education, whether the segregation occurs by law or by
fact."[6] But it could hardly escape notice that, whatever the
damage done to the white and the affluent, their academic
performance was not affected, as black children's was, nor
that the white and the affluent had rarely complained about
their isolation in the schools, or been the object of such great
solicitude on the part of the authorities. Some judges, and
some scholars, and a few white parents, might emphasize the
damage done white children by racial segregation, but that
damage was not "the problem."

The demand for integration came, therefore, to be seen as

fundamentally insulting. This, too, might have been predicted. In 1966, commenting on the then newly enacted Massachusetts Racial Imbalance Law, which held that any school with more than 50 per cent Negro (non-white was the official language) enrollment was in violation of the law, I suggested that

> I can easily foresee the time when (such remedies) will have outlived their remedial utility, when separating the Negro out as a special case, to be treated differently from all our other groups, will seem ridiculous. I can foresee, too, that there may come a day on which the Negro will himself insist that separation is not inherently unequal. . . . When it will be possible for a Negro . . . to go to school with other Negroes—or (with whomever) he chooses—then the Negroes will have come into their own.[7]

That was 1966. Within a year, the doctrine that Negroes can only perform at par when placed in white environments had come to be more widely perceived as insulting. One need only imagine such a doctrine—couched, of course, in appropriate and acceptable language—attached to any other major ethnic group to understand the ensuing protest. Indeed, in Massachusetts, where the Racial Imbalance Law spoke of "non-whites," one of the very first problems it created was with Boston's Chinese community. That community, long accustomed to nonintegrated schooling for its children, was not about to accept the dispersal of its children the law required. After making its position known, it was happily exempted from the provisions of the law, via the device of not counting Chinese as non-white.

Hence blacks were subjected simultaneously to the injury of continued segregation and to the insult of continued liberal insistence that only through integration could the educational failures of black children be repaired. Liberals approached the issue with decent intent, but despite their motives, the chief result of their activity was to add the insult to the injury.

And all this at a time when, for associated reasons, the

traditional civil rights movement was beginning to turn from a universal alliance based on the premise that the color of a man's skin is irrelevant, to a particular movement based on the premise that blackness is a resource.

Liberalism and Race

The traditional liberal perspective of the "race problem" has been—and, in important respects, continues to be—that Negroness is irrelevant, an accident with no intrinsic social meaning. The ideal society, according to this perception, is the color-blind society; the society in which there is no significant association between color and any valued status. This seems a noble perception, however difficult it has proved to persuade the mass of Americans of its validity. And it conforms quite precisely to more general liberal dogmas about the shape of the American future and the centrality of the unfettered individual to that future. The brotherhood of man, though it might be for the time being a utopian ideal, is nonetheless a powerful dream, deeply embedded in Christian ethic and widely diffused among men of diverse political persuasions. It is a dream which specifically excludes private fraternities smaller than the whole family of man.

Such an ideal might be expected to have particular appeal to Negroes themselves, for what could be more rewarding a destiny or more sustaining a hope than that color would come to lose its bite? The ideal of full racial equality is thus achieved when white Americans cease to penalize black Americans on account of color, when the unhappy correlations between blackness and poverty, blackness and infant mortality, blackness and crime, blackness and slums, are shattered, when Negroes take their place in the social order, among the rich and the poor, among the well and the sick, independent of their color.

On this point, as on few others, the liberal goal has been explicit, whether stated by whites or by blacks. Thus, Louis Lomax in 1963:

> Groupness . . . is the mortal enemy of democracy. It is
> mandatory that Americans of all ethnic backgrounds
> submerge their group loyalties in favor of the broad
> human values that undergird the democratic concept.
> This, to be sure, will take time; no one expects it to
> occur overnight. What we Negroes do expect, however
> —and now—is an announcement of this basic goal for
> American democracy.[8]

> And, as if in response, Lyndon Johnson in 1965:
> Most Americans remain true to our goal: the develop-
> ment of a national society in which the color of a man's
> skin is as irrelevant as the color of his eyes.[9]

Now it is reasonably clear that if we are to move towards
a society in which white people come to disregard blackness,
we must be able to assume that black men, too, will disregard blackness. For if they perceive it, and act upon it, if they
make it matter, then whites will not be able to ignore it. If
Negroes, for example, were to continue to prefer to associate
primarily with other Negroes, or were to insist on preserving
their special dialect, or, becoming scholars, were to specialize
in African studies, then we should be forced to recognize that
color does matter, and, therefore, that liberal, individually
oriented equality has not yet come about. Liberals, in short,
cannot accept the possibility that Negroes might, in truth,
have a sense of rhythm, much less that Negroes might want to
preserve some apartness, given a genuinely free choice.

Here and there, liberals have had the courage to follow
their convictions to their most logical conclusion, eloquently
stated by Norman Podhoretz:

> And when I think about the Negroes in America and
> about the image of integration as a state in which the
> Negroes would take their rightful place as another of
> the protected minorities in a pluralistic society, I
> wonder whether they really believe in their hearts that
> such a state can actually be attained, and if so *why*
> they should wish to survive as a distinct group. I think
> I know why the Jews once wished to survive (though I

am less certain as to why we still do): they not only believed that God has given them no choice, but they were tied to a memory of past glory and a dream of imminent redemption. What does the American Negro have that might correspond to this? *His past is a stigma, his color is a stigma, and his vision of the future is hope of erasing the stigma by making color irrelevant,* by making it disappear as a fact of consciousness. (Italics mine.) I share this hope, but I cannot see how it will ever be realized unless color does *in fact* disappear: and that means not integration, it means assimilation, it means—let the brutal word come out—miscegenation. . . . I believe that the wholesale merging of the two races is the most desirable alternative for everyone concerned.[10]

The Podhoretz statement offended many people when it was first published; it would surely offend many more today, at a time when the past he saw as an unmitigated stigma has come to be widely studied and celebrated. Its chief virtue was surely not accuracy, but, instead, consistency. For if color, as so many had so energetically argued, was irrelevant, then it followed that either people should be color-blind—the traditional approach—or, outrageously but literally: that they should be colorless.

Most people, of course, have avoided serious discussion of racial intermarriage, even when the logic of their position has suggested it quite directly. Instead, they have been content to argue the case for integration as a more immediate, more attainable, and, obviously, less volatile goal. Programmatically, liberals have operated on two fronts simultaneously. On the one hand, they have sought to combat the benighted prejudices of white Americans, while, on the other, they sought to "prepare" Negroes for integration, by teaching them the things that discrimination had, presumably, prevented them from learning. The two tactics were reinforcing; if blacks did not behave distinctively, whites could more easily become color-blind. If whites were less bigoted, blacks would not be "forced" to act distinctively.

Such an approach had, in fact, been successfully implemented in the case of the great immigrant groups that arrived in America between 1880 and 1920, and, while most recognized the special difficulties in the path of the "Americanization" of the Negro, the effort seemed a plausible one. In effect, liberal America's argument held that society was required to accept the black man, if only he did not insist upon his own blackness, if only, in other words, he were not too black. The distinctive characteristics of Negroes as a social group, largely negative in any case, would have to be suppressed so that Negroes, along with other liberated Americans, might seek their salvation as individuals, unstigmatized by such atavistic attributes as race.

Many Negroes responded to the liberal program and took elaborate steps to straighten their hair, lighten their skin, adjust their behavior.[11] That standards of beauty within the Negro community were caucasian was one fact among many reflecting the dominance of white models.

We were witness, during the heyday of Negro "adjustment," to the effects of two different phenomena. On the one hand, maligned minority groups tend to accept the negative stereotypes with which others view them. They came, thereby, to devalue themselves and their own qualities. On the other hand, liberal Americans, in pursuit both of justice for the Negro and of liberal ideals, promised that Negroes would be accepted, if, among other things that had to happen, they would stop being Negroes. There was, therefore, both a push and a pull towards white standards and white behaviors.

Once again, we cannot know what might have been, if Negroes had more assiduously adopted—or had been permitted to adopt—the majority culture. For, once again, white America did not respond as liberals had hoped it would. While liberals promised to welcome the black man if only he was not too black, most white Americans continued to see only the blackness and not the man. And the powerful drive of the late 1950's and 1960's, in which national attention was mercilessly riveted on the special hardships and penalties imposed on Negroes, simply reinforced the conviction of many whites that Negroes were, in fact, special. Moreover, lower middle class America, with whom, after all, it was most plausible to suppose that Negroes would, if at all, be integrated, had never been especially impressed with the individualist doctrines of liberalism. On the contrary, lower middle class America was, and is, in many of its parts, ethnic America, that part of America which still takes both comfort and pride in the special attributes of roots and of groups.[12] The peculiar coalition of affluent liberals and underclass blacks could not speak for, and barely spoke to, the object of its egalitarian assault.

Negro Responses

Negroes who reflected on such matters, as a rising generation of educated Negroes no doubt did, could easily reach three conclusions: first, while there might be many negative aspects to Negro life in America, it was by no means clear that white society was morally superior. If, after all the intense pressure and all the appeals to conscience, white Americans still resisted integration and still effectively condoned outrage, then white society must be deeply flawed. For just as oppressed minorities come to believe what their oppressors say about them, so, too, if they are blessed, do they come to realize that they are, in at least one critical respect, superior to their oppressors—that is, they themselves are not oppressors. The two beliefs, in fact, are not discrepant. Self-hatred does not necessarily preclude disdain of others.

Second, liberal America could not speak for white America. And third, even liberal America, despite its sensitivity, persisted in the belief that *it* was the appropriate guardian of the gate, that its very liberalness entitled it to assert the terms of black acceptability.

Add the stark demographic facts of America's leading

urban centers (increasingly black in their composition, still more black in their school populations), and integration, even if valued, even if accepted, became mechanically impossible in some cities, overwhelmingly difficult in others.

It is not surprising, therefore, that many Negro leaders came to question the utility of integration as a proximate goal. The whole concept of integration was simply too problematic, both theoretically and practically, to sustain those who had accepted its logic at a time when it seemed to imply simply the removal of legal barriers to equality.

Accordingly, the insight of Booker T. Washington, long rejected as demeaning by white and black liberals alike, that "In all things that are purely social we can be as separate as the fingers, yet one as the hand in all things essential to mutual progress," came to be seen as an acceptable doctrine. If integration were to be denied, Negroes could not afford to believe that only through integration would the disorganization of Negro life come to an end. Hence attention turned to the internal development of the Negro community. If the one-by-one integration of Negroes into the society, in numbers small enough not to threaten whites and only as Negroes met certain (white-defined) criteria of acceptability, was the best that could be expected, an alternative theory of the good society had to be developed, a more plausible, a more approachable, and a more palatable theory.

The central feature of such a theory had to be that Negroes were not, after all, dependent upon integration, that if they could find the appropriate tools, they could fashion a positive community regardless of white stereotype. There were various ways in which this approach might be rationalized, none without problems, and each found some adherents:

1. The chief aspects of Negro life are not, in fact, dysfunctional; instead, they are highly functional adaptations to external circumstance. Whites choose to define them as negative simply because they differ from white forms. Since even when blacks debase themselves by imitating white be-

haviors whites remain, on the whole, unimpressed, and hostile to integration, there is no sensible reason for rejecting the more natural patterns. Thus:

> . . . In the American ethos a black man is not only 'different,' he is classed as ugly and inferior.
> This is not an easy situation to deal with, and the manner in which a Negro chooses to handle it will be both determined by and a determinant of his larger political outlook. He can deal with it as an integrationist, accepting his child as being ugly by prevailing standards and urging him to excel in other ways to prove his worth; or he can deal with it as a black nationalist, telling the child that he is not a freak but rather part of a larger international community of black-skinned, kinky-haired people who have a beauty of their own, a glorious history, and a great future.[13]

Or,

> There is . . . a certain kind of beauty in those young Negroes—80,000 of them in New York City—who cannot get work. Mayor Lindsay knows they cannot get work. The statistics prove they cannot get work. The Freedom Budget has not been passed. So what do they do? They live by their wits, selling numbers, and selling marijuana, and other things. Now, if I say that's 'soul,' you'll say to me, 'but Mr. Rustin, that's illegal stuff, and even dope.' But there's a certain amount of grit, and determination on their part not to hit bottom, to get some of the things that life says they should have.[14]

Insofar as this position reflects a conscious effort to break loose from the debilitating legacy of self-hatred, it is both plausible and persuasive. But social doctrines are never dispensed with scientific precision, and the doctrine that "black is beautiful" is, therefore, liable to be taken to mean that "only black is beautiful," or that "everything black is beautiful." Neither over-reaction is especially common, although one encounters both from time to time, especially in the rhetoric of some white radicals. Among the central black spokesmen of black power, the identity and self-help themes are much more central.[15]

2. White society itself is sick, and Negroes ought not want to become a part of it. In all versions, white sickness is manifest especially in its continuing racism, and also in America's behavior in Viet Nam. In some versions, the sickness is a necessary adjunct to capitalism. How can Negroes choose a way of life—even were the choice permitted—to which rejection of the Negro has been so central?

This position has a decidedly sour grapes undertone, as it can be argued that if white society is, at last, prepared to "accept" Negroes, it is in the process of healing its own sickness. But those who have despaired of all decency in white society, at least at the institutional level, are attracted by its logic. Moreover, this position is central to white radicals, and constitutes, thereby, a reasonable basis for alliance, whatever the state of its credibility.

3. Negroes have been too dependent on white good will, which has proved a superficial, or, at least, insufficient resource. They ought to be more dependent on their own resources. Their resources, in addition to their shared experience, include especially their concentrated numbers in important urban centers, hence their capacity to affect white society, including their capacity to make life difficult unless their demands are met. Instead of exploiting the often maudlin guilt of small numbers of white liberals, they might instead exploit the deeply entrenched fears of the masses of whites.

This argument, which requires a high level of mobilization and organization, would likely have been difficult to translate into an operational doctrine save for the advent of the Community Action Program, which gave legitimacy—and some subsidy, as well—to community organization at a critical ideological moment.

4. Finally, white liberals, in dealing with the issue of race,

have invoked a standard to which white society itself does not at all conform. For Negroes to seek individual integration, rather than group cohesion, would be to respond to a liberal perception which has little to do with the way Americans, in fact, behave. For America is a collection of groups, not of individuals, no matter how much liberals might wish it otherwise. Upper middle class America does not speak for, and cannot deliver, lower middle class America, yet it is lower middle class America, given white and Negro income distributions, which is asked to accept blacks. If this situation is to be confronted at all, lower middle class America will have to be met on its own terms, which are, substantially, ethnic terms.

The obvious problem with this argument is tactical: the logic of the liberal ethic suggests that ethnic organization is subversive. Therefore, to organize along ethnic lines means to threaten the liberal dogma, and hence to lose liberals as allies. The response, of course, is that the earlier alliances did not seem to be getting anywhere.

These and other doctrines, despite their problematic aspects, are all accepted, to some degree, as preferable to what has come to be interpreted by a significant number of black leaders as the pernicious doctrine of integration. It is quite troublesome for whites, and for white liberals in particular, to understand why the ideal of integration should, as an ideal, have fallen on such dark days. (As a reality, its status is less clear.) Many had supposed that positive programs for integration were simply extensions of earlier efforts at desegregation. Yet there is a major difference between the two. Desegregation is an effort to repair a failure of the white community, to undo a senseless and evil behavior. Integration, presented as the only means by which Negroes might truly achieve equality, in effect seeks to repair an alleged failure of Negroes. It was unthinkable that a community could for very long accept the information (a) that it was badly diseased, (b) that there was only one medicine which would cure the disease, and (c) that the medicine would not be made available. Since there seemed to be no way in which the needed medicine could be pried loose, some rejected, or, at least, sought to modify, the diagnosis, and more still sought to discover a different medicine. That is why Stokely Carmichael could say that

> Integration speaks to the problem of blackness in a despicable way. As a goal, it has been based on a complete acceptance of the fact that *in order to have* a decent house or education, blacks must move into a white neighborhood or send their children to a white school. This reinforces, among both black and white, the idea that 'white' is automatically better and 'black' is by definition inferior. This is why integration is a subterfuge for the maintenance of white supremacy.[16]

What Carmichael, and others, failed to recognize was that the whites who favored integration were trapped not by their sinister racism, but by their liberal ethic itself, by an ethic which only a few years earlier had seemed both enlightened and responsible, and even now, remains central to the American liberal tradition.*

This is, admittedly, only one among several possible ways of reading the events of recent years, and it leaves out major aspects of the story. The full story would have to include not only the continuing lack of integration, but also the very significant economic progress that Negroes have made since 1960, the bitter competition for power within a black community in which power has come to have a vastly expanded meaning, the movement away from concern with individual bigotry to concern with institutionalized racism, and much more. The effort here is not to present comprehensive detail, but to interpret a mood which has led to the demand for community control of the schools. That demand was also hastened by a rather separate issue, the issue of the quality and organization of American education in the 1950's and 1960's.

---

* See Chapter Two for a fuller discussion of the "liberal dilemma."

The Issue of Decentralization

Criticism of public education is a national pastime for Americans. Recently, one of the more popular objects of that criticism has been the over-centralized, over-bureaucratized, urban school system. The most direct explanation for the concern with centralization is the relative success of some suburban systems when compared to most of the large urban systems. Since the most apparent difference between the two is in size, it is easy to conclude that smaller systems are better. (In fact, if we pass over Negro performance in urban systems and include among small systems working class and rural areas, the differences are negligible.) The conclusion is bolstered by the special case of New York City, with its gargantuan school system, including, as it does, over 50,000 teachers and over a million students.

Efforts to decentralize the New York school system began at least as far back as 1933. Reports calling for one form of decentralization or another were issued in that year, again in 1942, in 1949, in 1962, in 1965, in 1967, and in 1968.[17] And the dates refer only to the public documents, not to the steady volume of journalistic and scholarly writing in the area. The earlier versions emphasized the barriers to innovation to which the hugeness of the system gave rise. Decentralization was seen purely as an administrative reform, designed to achieve greater efficiency and flexibility.

In the more recent versions, a new note is added, which eventually becomes the central motif. That is the note of participation. *Reconnection for Learning* (the Bundy Report), presented in 1967 by the Mayor's Advisory Panel on Decentralization of the New York City Schools, recalls the earlier proposals when it holds that

> The causes of the decline (of the New York City school system) are as diverse and complex as the school system itself and the city that created it. But one critical fact is that the bulk and complexity of the system have gravely weakened the ability to act of all concerned—

teachers, parents, supervisors, the Board of Education, and local school boards.[18]

But the report later asserts that earlier efforts at decentralization in New York had been ineffective because they had been basically administrative in character. What is required, in the Panel's judgment, is more direct participation in decision making by local groups, and especially by parents, since "parents can be trusted to care more than anyone else for the quality of the education their children get."[19] Hence the title "Reconnection for Learning," and hence the statement "the central purpose of (the Panel's) recommendations is to reconnect all the parties of New York so that each will have more constructive power."[20]

The notion that a community-based school system has direct educational value, beyond even the simplification of lines of authority—the notion, for example, that children may learn better if their parents are directly involved in their education—is a serious idea put forward by serious people, and, even if the Bundy Report does not itself provide a wholly convincing statement of the rationale, there is a growing body of literature which makes the linkages between community participation and student performance quite explicit. Yet, it is likely that many who read *of* the Report, but failed to read *in* it, assumed that its logic was entirely the earlier reformist logic, since the principle of administrative reform has both a longer history and a simpler underlying theory.

Accordingly, the coalition of proponents of decentralization for the New York system included both those whose essential purpose was administrative reform and those who sought more fundamental political restructuring. For the first group, the major benefits would accrue from making a too-big system smaller; for the second, the benefits lay in increasing popular participation in the system.

The two views are not necessarily in conflict; neither, however, are they necessarily linked. For though all who seek political restructuring also support administrative reform, not all who support administrative reform favor political restructuring. And the differences between the two, proceeding as they do from two entirely different theoretical propositions, were never made entirely clear to members of the supporting coalition. One can speculate that the reason for the obscurity was that the authors of the movement for decentralization were themselves not clear about the differences (although the Bundy Report seems to take note of them), or that managers of the coalition were anxious to build the broadest possible base of support for their proposals, and hence sought to avoid making internal differences explicit. In the Fall of 1968, in the wake of events in the Ocean Hill-Brownsville experimental school district, public education in New York City simply collapsed. Whatever the full explanation for the debacle, a major cause was clearly that some of the members of the pro-decentralization coalition were taken by surprise when they discovered that the changes they had endorsed involved actual control of the schools by local communities. They had agreed, as it were, to produce a play, but when the curtain went up on opening night the characters were reading from a different script—a script the producers would not have endorsed and felt they had never been shown.

This book is not about the New York City schools.[21] But because no school crisis has been so profound or so dramatic, and because those who have followed that crisis in the press may themselves be unaware of the differences between administrative decentralization and community control—that is, between a simple theory of organization and a complex theory of education—it is necessary to make clear that our concern is with community control, and not with mere administrative decentralization, except as it is implied by community control.

It is also important, as a matter of history, to note that the proponents of community control in New York, the nation's most visible stage, were able to take advantage of the traditional bloc of support for decentralization in that city, gaining thereby a critical political advantage without which their efforts might have come to naught. For precisely to the degree to which the public failed to distinguish between decentralization and community control, the position of the supporters of community control seemed eminently respectable, even conventional, certainly non-threatening, well within the tradition of debate over public education. (Hence later, when the differences became painfully clear, some members of the earlier coalition felt they had been betrayed, which helped to convert a serious policy question into an intensely personal dispute.)

Further, although there were other reasons for fixing on the schools as the primary target of community control, and although other areas of life—the police, commercial enterprise, municipal services—were also seen as appropriate objects for community control, the primary reason that events unfolded so quickly in the case of the schools was that there, more than anywhere else, there seemed to be a plausible claim on the educational tradition itself. Note that the Bundy Report was entitled "*Re*connection," suggesting that at some earlier time the called for connections were there. Curiously, however, the pages of general educational criticism during the past several years are virtually bare of any endorsement of community control as a solution. Except when the problem addressed is the education of Negroes, or when the authors write not specifically about education but in endorsement of participatory democracy in general, community control is simply not mentioned.

On the contrary, the dominant view of educational critics, at least of liberal persuasion, over the past decade, was expressed quite well by Myron Lieberman when he suggested that "The public interest is almost invariably better served by leaving professional questions to the professionals. . . ."[22] Local control results in the same kind of intellectual protectionism that characterizes schools in totalitarian countries."[23] At the time when Lieberman was writing, critics of public education were particularly concerned with issues of censorship growing out of the McCarthy period, with problems of desegregation growing out of the 1954 Supreme Court decision, and with problems of quality brought into focus by Sputnik. In all three cases, it seemed clear that the barrier to reform was the persistence of local control.

If, however, the schools were locally controlled in 1958, then they were locally controlled in 1968. No revolution took place during the decade. Hence, when Mario Fantini, Executive Secretary of the staff on the Bundy Report, argues that "Once upon a time, the people created public schools, and the schools belonged to them," and now, at last, "the public is seeking to repossess its schools,"[24] one is entitled to grow somewhat restless. Either local control, which Lieberman eschews, and community control, which Fantini endorses, do not mean the same thing, or somebody has his history confused. For Lieberman says we have it, and shouldn't, while Fantini says we don't have it, and should.

It is likely that the two terms do not mean precisely the same thing. It is also likely that those supporters of community control who seek to place it in the mainstream of the American educational tradition know better, which is to say that they know that there never was a time in industrial America when schools in urban areas were definitively controlled by the local community, much less the neighborhood. The tension between professional judgment and community values has been part of the story of American public education at least since educators began to view themselves (and, occasionally, to be viewed by others) as professionals. And, in general, history has favored the professionals. Certainly, intellectual critics (themselves, of course, professionals) have been overwhelmingly on the side of the professionals.

There was, indeed, a time when communities had more to say about how their children were to be educated. It was not so much a time when *schools* were more subject to community control as it was a time when *extra-school* educational inputs were more systematic and more manageable. In pre-urban, and pre-liberal, and especially in pre-television

America, parents could and did feel more confident that the established institutions were effectively transmitting their own values to the young. But tasks once assumed by the family and church have now passed, by and large, to the mass media, and parents have little control over the stimuli to which their children are thereby exposed. So much so that one may regard genuine community efforts to retain (or to reassert) control over the schools as a last-ditch effort to retain some control over the education of the young, an effort directed at the schools not because they are the traditional transmission belts of community values but simply because the school is the only educative institution that remains, to some degree, vulnerable to direct political pressure. But this is obviously not what intellectual endorsers of community control are talking about. For intellectuals, far from lamenting the erosion of parochial influence on the schools, have been wholly committed to secular education, and hence to the increasing nationalization of the curriculum content of the schools. So, at least, until they came to deal with the education of black children.

If, then, we are now confronted with a claim that community control is an important educational reform, we must see and assess the reform as a proposed innovation, not as an effort to reclaim a lost heritage. The assertion that community control is such an effort must be seen as arising out of the specific problem of educating Negroes, and the need, therefore, to recruit allies for the proposed reform.

That is not to say that community control is not an authentic, nor a reasonable, nor even a beneficent proposal. But it is a proposal that needs to be examined on its merits and not in the context of nostalgic rhetoric. It is a proposal which grows out of a specific educational problem, and not, at least in the first instance, out of a concern for the state of education in general. (Indeed, as we shall see, one of the most aggravating circumstances of the effort is that community control is an urgent question only with respect to black communities, and may, in fact, be a plausible solution only for them. But the system is, in some ways, color-blind after all, and cannot easily move towards community control for blacks without moving towards it for everyone.)

It is sometimes argued that the effort by black communities to achieve control over their schools is no more than an effort to achieve what whites already have. In its most reasoned form the argument holds that Negroes are blocked from living in suburbs, where good education occurs in America; that suburban education is decisively community controlled; that central city black communities are penalized doubly—once by being forced to live where they live and once by being prevented, where they are forced to live, from managing their own lives.

This is a powerful argument, but it has very little to do with the quality of education, since (a) any number of central city schools not community controlled produce very able students, or, at least, are attended by able students, and (b) any number of suburban schools, notably those in non-affluent communities, do not produce very able students at all.

The argument, then, suggests merely what must by now be clear: the urge towards community control over the schools is not based solely on educational theory. It involves, centrally, if not equally, social and political theories as well. And it is these to which we now turn.

CHAPTER TWO

COMMUNITY CONTROL AS SOCIAL THEORY

Liberalism and Community

WE CANNOT simply conclude, as some parties to the New York City dispute seem to have concluded, that all those who oppose community control are racists, while all those who support it are men of good will. It is too easy to so dismiss the opposition. The noise of the debate ought not to obscure the very serious problems the issue raises for those who have traditionally been on the side of both educational reform and civil rights. The issue of community control raises very special problems for liberal intellectuals, for it challenges the basic assumptions of liberal doctrine. In particular, it raises questions concerning what the word "community" means, and ought to mean, in America. For many liberals, the doctrine of community control, far from recalling a lost and happy time, seems to threaten the very core of the liberal understanding of society; worse yet, it raises, quite volubly, an issue most had supposed long since settled.

For the issue of community is not new to intellectual concern. It has been a central concept—and problem—in Western social and political thought from the very earliest times. As far back as one looks one finds social critics both observing the erosion of community and lamenting its loss. Thus, Cicero complained that

> Maritime cities are . . . exposed to corrupt influences, and revolutions of manners. Their civilization is more or less adulterated by new language and customs, and they import not only foreign merchandise, but also foreign fashions, which allow not fixation or consolidation of the institutions of such cities. Those who inhabit these maritime towns do not remain in their native place, but are urged far from their homes by winged hope and speculation. And even when they do not desert their country in person, their minds are always expatiating and voyaging round the world.[1]

The argument is sometimes difficult to follow because the vocabulary is highly unstable. Tradition, community, rationality, secularization, the sacred, folk—these are just a few of the words that have been used to describe the ends of a continuum about which countless philosophers and would-be philosophers have written. But if by community we intend a set of relationships which are fundamentally organic rather than contractual, then it is clear that almost all commentators believe the modern era (which is to say, the era in which the philosopher writes) to be profoundly hostile to community. The typical villain is technological modernization—in Cicero's time, the growth of oceanic transportation, in our time, first the automobile and, more latterly and more sinisterly, television. From Disraeli ("modern society acknowledges no neighbor") to Weber ("secularization and its concomitant rationalization may be good, or it may be bad, but it is our destiny")[2] to David Riesman ("the lonely crowd") the fact has been accepted, no matter what the evaluation.

No matter what the evaluation. The central conclusion of conservative theory has been that the loss of community is a desperately and tragically serious loss. Since the Enlightenment, which purposefully sought to subvert traditional bases of association, and since the French Revolution, which rent the traditional fabric, conservatives have argued that the dissolution of community would issue (or had already issued) in disaster.

Their fears were echoed even by those who, unlike most of the conservatives, saw no possibility of reversing the process. Maitland and Maine, Weber and Tonnies, and others who identified the process variously as a transition from folk society to urban society, from *gemeinschaft* to *gesselschaft,* from status to contract, from tradition to rationality, from particularism to universalism, joined in the conservative concern that without community man would be diminished rather than, as the Enlightenment had argued, enlarged.

American social and political doctrine is ambivalent in its evaluation of community. The myth of the small town, with its splendid fraternity and diverse associated virtues, is writ large in our past and our institutions. Indeed, much of what passes for social criticism in America is essentially the expression of a profound suspicion of cities on the grounds that urban life encourages anonymity and selfishness, and thereby subverts the dispositions popular democracy requires in order to survive.[3] Josiah Strong said that "The first city was built by the first murderer, and crime and vice and wretchedness have festered in it ever since," and many Americans would have no quarrel with this.

At the same time, and rather more powerfully, the American myth has extolled the individual, whether he be the sturdy yeoman of New England, the rugged frontiersman of the West, or the industrial tycoon of the Horatio Alger stories. In a continent which was to be made rather than inherited, in which there was hardly community to lose, individual freedom became the fundamental precept. And the bias of liberal intellectuals, despite their suspicion of the city and their sometime nostalgia for small-town virtue, was quite decisively on the side of man's break with the bonds of tradition, of his movement towards total rationality.

What Rollo May has called the "myth of the mythless

society," an understanding derived largely from the Enlightenment, speaks of a good society based on man's liberation: his liberation from nature, achieved through science; his liberation from bondage, achieved through law; his liberation from self, achieved through psychoanalysis; his liberation from the dead hand of the past, achieved through commitment to change; his liberation from the confines of time and space, achieved through intellectual and physical mobility; his liberation from myth itself, achieved through education.

If community means, as it has to most liberal intellectuals, a set of arational, mystical, inherited, particularistic commitments, then community is incompatible with liberal utopia. Community is seen as an impediment to freedom; while community may promote stability, stability itself is stifling. Man, in his full power, must learn to live with freedom without the crutch of community or myth.

These are, of course, normative statements, and one might have supposed that the debate between those who prefer myth to modernity and those who choose, say, freedom over friendship, might have proceeded, as debates over values presumably do, with neither side able to claim victory for its position. At one level, indeed, the debate has remained essentially normative, although it is difficult to find a recent spokesman for the conservative view as persuasive as Burke, or even Bagehot. But the normative doctrine of universalism has been enormously aided by the apparent weight of evidence in its favor—that is, by its conversion into an apparently descriptive theory, based not on values but on empirical data.

As description, the position that modernization inevitably requires secularization is now accepted by most social scientists, and especially by students of the process of modernization, as the following two quotations illustrate:

> Relationships among individuals (in small groups) are mainly *ascribed* (fixed by birth or other involuntary membership), *diffuse* (covering a wide and open-ended range of rights and duties), and *particularistic* (based on particular relations to particular persons or statuses,

not on generalized, impersonal rules). In modern complex societies, the four basic structures (kinship, territorial community, social stratification, and ethnic grouping) are interlaced and overlaid by economic and political systems that are organized in considerable part as radically different principles—the principle of achieved, competitive placement rather than ascription by birth, of impersonal universalistic norms, and of highly specific, narrowly defined relations among persons. Also, in our society (the United States), the major religious traditions all stress universalism in the ethical domain.[4] . . . The passage from 'traditional' to 'modern' society . . . involves a complex set of changes in the organization of society and in man's perspective on his society. There is a movement from identification with primary groups to identification with secondary groups, from social norms in which status is derived from inherited place in the order (ascription) to the function that one performs in society and how well one performs it (achievement). It is a movement towards more complex, highly differentiated and specialized social institutions and social roles. Life becomes less viewed as a whole, less diffuse, within the setting of the village and traditional agriculture. . . . Modern society (similarly) requires a different sort of political order, one serviceable to a much expanded notion of the relevant community, as the scope of social life changes from the order of the village to the order of the nation.[5]

These statements take the form of descriptive theory, value-neutral and ideology-free. Whether or not they, and a hundred others like them, are accurate as description is beside the present point, which is simply that American culture is not at all neutral towards the terms they use: the culture rejects relationships which are "fixed by birth or other involuntary membership," endorses "impersonal rules" (a government of laws, not of men), and welcomes "universalism." Most of all, the culture supports modernity, a tomorrow more free of the past than based on it. And if social scientists, in their wisdom, assert as a matter of fact that modernity requires the dissolution of tradition, they effectively subvert the conservative position, which must necessarily be seen as an anti-progress position. Unfortunately, the spokesman of tradition are themselves implicated in the victory of modernity, for they tend to argue their case in Luddite terms, thereby implying acceptance of the fundamental proposition of modernism—to wit, that high technology and tradition are incompatible.

Social scientists have thereby become priests for the prophetic tenets of liberalism. One can speculate endlessly about the actual freedom from value commitments with which contemporary social scientists proceed in their diagnoses. My own judgment is that the enthusiasm with which they welcome the concomitants of modernization goes well beyond the somewhat reluctant *rapprochement* with the inevitable which characterized earlier scholars. With but an occasional nostalgic nod to the past, the future is more nearly pursued than merely accepted. As Robert Nisbet has pointed out,

> To regard all evil as a persistence or revival of the past has been a favorite conceit of liberals nourished by the idea of Progress. . . . Present evils could safely be regarded as regrettable evidences of incomplete emancipation from the past—from tribalism, from agrarianism, religion, localism, and the like. In one form or another, the theory of culture lag has been the secular approach to the problem of evil.[6]

Or,

> The demands of freedom appeared to be in the direction of the release of large numbers of individuals from the statuses and identities that had been forged in them by the dead hand of the past. A free society would be one in which individuals were morally and socially as well as politically free, free from groups and classes. . . . Freedom would arise from the individual's release from all the inherited personal interdependencies of traditional community, and from his existence in an impersonal, natural, economic order.[7]

It is, in short, rather difficult to know just when we are dealing with a purely normative doctrine and when we are dealing with pure description. It seems reasonable to conclude, however, that the description, pure or not in its genesis, has come to be interpreted as an ideology.

Now it might seem that decades of experience with the recalcitrance of parochial loyalties would have subverted the liberal commitment, at the very least forcing liberals to ask more sensitively what the functions of tradition were for those who have clung so desperately to it. We do, in fact, find a number of serious scholars who grapple valiantly with the recurring evidence of the urge to community, and an even larger literature which expresses skepticism about man's capacity to cope with the new freedom.[8] But the evidence of man's reluctance to assume the burden of rationality, or to relinquish the alleged atavism of community, is typically taken to show that we still have a long way to go, that the liberal proselytization has not been sufficiently aggressive, rather than that we may be going in the wrong direction. At the level of popularized liberal doctrine, the stance remains, despite all, thoroughly optimistic:

> Human beings throughout the world are fundamentally alike. They share a common anatomical structure; they have the ability to engage in reflective thought; and they share a pool of common sentiments. Hence, when social distance is reduced, individuals recognize their resemblances. The basic differences between ethnic groups are cultural, and conventional norms serve as masks to cover the similarities. Whenever men interact informally, the common human nature comes through. It would appear, then, that it is only a matter of time before a more enlightened citizenry will realize this. Then, there will be a realignment of group loyalties, and ethnic identity will become a thing of the past.[9]

It would be unfair to modern social science to suggest that it has been completely insensitive to the issue of community.

The more accurate statement is that social science has perceived a necessary conflict between the demands of community and the requirements of rationality, and, with more or less—typically less—regret about the decision, has chosen to insist on rationality. Commitment to the secular city as the liberal utopia is, of course, supported by the American myth of the melting pot, a myth which holds the private fraternity of groups within the whole not only anachronistic, but actually subversive.

In brief: there is a marked tension between the concept of community, which is based on non-rational considerations, and the concept of liberty, insofar as that concept has been defined in current social theory as dependent on total rationality. In general, American liberals (meaning, incidentally, most American social scientists) have taken their stand on the side of rationality, and, therefore, against community.[10] Where liberals have countenanced the concept of community at all, their embrace has been limited to what Morris Janowitz calls "the community of limited liability," a community based either on shared taste, or on shared neighborhood, or on a shared specific and limited interest.[11] This is quite different from the diffuse organic community, based as much on mystique as on reason, acting as primary group to its members, speaking a private language. The organic community, best represented in the American experience by immigrant ethnic groups, and, occasionally, by small towns, has been explicitly and often vehemently rejected as an anachronism.

Liberalism, Negroes, and Community

The special case of the Negro American is—or was—easily dealt with by conventional liberal theory. So long as blackness remained relevant in determining a man's destiny, so long was universalism delayed. Accordingly, liberals were required to seek the day when Negroes would be randomly distributed throughout the American society and economy, when there would be no significant statistical association between color and any other important variable. The "normalization" of the black condition could, then, be best measured by the deviation of Negroes from norms derived from the white experience.

Such a standard gives rise to two problems, one educational, the other theoretical. First, it is fairly clear that the chief barrier in the path of liberal enlightenment is the persistent inability of most Americans to ignore race as a defining category. Hence the major activity of liberals is to educate white Americans towards tolerance, and, ultimately, towards color-blindness. There are several different ways in which such education can be directed, and each has been employed at one time or another. The purely rational approach, in which learned scientists solemnly pronounce the irrelevance of race, was especially popular during the 1940's. During the 1950's, the gap between the American creed and American behavior (following Myrdal) was emphasized. The appeal to reason and the appeal to conscience was followed by an appeal to self-interest in which white society was cautioned of the social danger of continuing discrimination.

The results of these several assaults on private prejudice have not been trivial. With all the talk of backlash and racism, it must be borne in mind that a significant shift in expressed public opinion on race-related issues has taken place in the last twenty years, and the shift has been markedly in the direction of liberal enlightenment. Nonetheless, Negroes remain, in large part, an afflicted group in American society, and the costs of being born black, in terms of life expectancy, access to quality education and housing, health care, and income, remain intolerably high.

Quite likely as a result of frustration with the necessarily sluggish process of individual conversion, recent emphasis has shifted from individuals to institutions. The term "racism," popularized by the Kerner Commission (but nowhere defined by it) suggests a new, and somewhat more complex understanding, of the sources of discrimination.[12] For if "racism" means something different from "prejudice," it points towards a pattern of institutional discrimination, a discrimination, as it were, of habit and not of men. One can imagine a set of institutions managed by people of boundless goodwill and decency, behaving independently of the people who manage them. In large and efficient bureaucracies, people are interchangeable; it is the rules that govern. And if the rules have discriminatory consequences — especially if such consequences are unintended — then the fact that those who apply them are enlightened rather than benighted may make precious little difference. At best, the actors may interpret the script more humanely; it is far less likely that they have the authority—or the desire, or the capacity—to rewrite the script. It is especially difficult to engage in rewriting a script which has, in the main, proved praiseworthy in other respects. If, for example, we find that a merit system which, when instituted, was applauded as a great reform, now penalizes Negroes, reluctance to change the rules is understandable. Until very recently, no one questioned the assumption that removal of racial and religious quotas by institutions of higher education was a good thing. Now we have come to recognize that their replacement by a competitive merit system discriminates against Negroes. Hence there is some pressure to re-introduce a quota system, at least to deal with this one group. But a society which has prided itself on secularizing the rules by which its institutions live, which has sought to depersonalize bureaucratic behavior, can be expected to bridle at the change.

Hence it is not clear what actions will issue in a normalization of the Negro condition, nor, for that matter, whether proposed actions can be reconciled with other valued social goals. We know only that seeking such normalization through appeals to white people is, at best, a painfully tedious path to reform.

Beyond the question of tactics lies a more fundamental theoretical problem: how shall "normalization" be defined? At first blush, the traditional definition of randomness seems acceptable. According to this definition, the "Negro problem" will have been resolved when the distribution curves which describe such diverse phenomena as infant mortality, education, income, and occupational distribution for Negroes are indistinguishable from white distribution curves. This is a rather moderate goal; it holds acceptable, for example, continued poverty among Negroes, so long as the proportion of Negro poor does not exceed the proportion of white poor. It is, therefore, distinguishable from current radical demands which seek absolute equality (of individuals), rather than distributional equality (of groups).

But even the moderate goal of distributional equality, whose proximate justice seems so apparent, is in fact quite problematic. For the goal is only tenable so long as Negroes are viewed (and view themselves) as lacking any significant group characteristics. If such characteristics do exist—that is to say, if there is such a thing as a black culture, a culture with at least some positive properties (however defined)— then those characteristics will affect Negro performance, and will introduce a bias into the "ideal" of randomness.[13]

Suppose, for example, that the index under discussion is college attendance. If Negroes are simply people who happen to be black, then the ideal condition, according to the traditional definition, is one in which Negroes attend college in the same proportions as all whites. But if the black community has cultural attributes that lend meaning to blackness, then we should expect those attributes to affect the college attendance rate. We know that not all white groups attend college at the same rate. Whereas the figure for post-secondary education for the society as a whole is now at about forty per cent, over 80 percent of college-age Jews are in college, and substantially less than 40 percent of college-age Italians. To expect the Negro community to attend college at the average rate at which whites attend is to imply that Negroes somehow reflect an average which, for whites, is compounded of quite distinctive subcultural patterns. If, therefore, Negroes are themselves a subculture, then there is no reason to suppose that they will miraculously perform at arbitrary means. They may do "better" in some respects, "worse" in others; they will, over a series of measures, retain a distinctive pattern of performance.

The question then becomes whether the distinctive qualities of Negro performance derive from external constraint, as at present, or from internal (group) values. But that is not a question which can be answered with standard statistical techniques. It is a far more difficult question, and the answers to it are far more tentative, not to say contentious. Further, so long as subcultural deviations are expected, differences between black and white performance may incorrectly be attributed to such internally generated tendencies when in fact they issue from externally imposed barriers. It has always been a popular technique among bigots to blame the alleged failings of the groups they attack on the groups themselves rather than on their own hostility.

External discrimination remains so general today that it may be thought that the problem of distinguishing between such discrimination and legitimate subcultural patterns is a problem for the future. Yet the issue of whether Negro Americans are, as it were, entitled to be different—on their own terms—is very much with us. Further, the new militancy, impatient with guarantees of equal opportunity which it finds difficult to believe, increasingly insists that the only valid evidence that opportunities are, in fact as well as in theory, equal, is whether results are equal. Returning to the illustration of college admissions, the argument is now put forward that protestations by colleges that they do not discriminate are credible only if colleges can in fact point to a black enrollment roughly proportionate to the number of potential black students in the community. Hence, at one and the same time we are confronted with a powerful appeal to the traditional ethic—measure equality by proportionality—and an emphasis on community, which suggest the likelihood of non-proportionality based on community idiosyncracy.

Liberal doctrine necessarily prefers the former measure, since it is based on the liberal ethic. It is also a less ambitious ethic, since it is capable of being measured quite precisely. But liberal guilt over white failings, including the inability of liberals to reform the white community, creates a fundamental ambivalence in assessing the new emphasis on community and subculture. The typical reconciliation of the tension between randomness and community as goals is the belief that we must move rapidly to "outgrow" the fundamentally anachronistic urge towards community. In this view —a view encountered among many Negro leaders as well as white liberals—the assertion of community is a necessary first step towards eventual integration, defined in the traditional universalistic manner.

Many liberals, however, remain thoroughly committed to the secular city and accept as axiomatic that society ought to be an aggregate of independent individuals rather than an organic compact of groups. Such a view necessarily points to a polity in which all legitimate authority is vested in the State.[14] Assertions that a "sacred" entity, such as an organic community, should be viewed as a legitimate partner to the embracing secular authority threaten not only the institutions of liberal society but its assumptions as well.[15] The call for community control is hardly less a challenge to these assumptions than attacks against the separation of church and state —which, interestingly, we now witness more frequently than a decade ago.

Were we not dealing with Negroes, but with some other ethnic community, the battle would be far more intense, for liberals would almost certainly act with vigor against the perceived threat to their core value commitment. It takes only memory, not imagination, to visualize the intensity of liberal hostility to parochial management of the schools, whether the parochialism is expressed by Southerners opposed to integration, Rotarians opposed to the *New Republic,* or Catholics committed to prayer in the schools. Once again, we may cite Myron Lieberman's expression of what was clearly the dominant liberal approach of the 1950's:

> National survival now requires educational policies and programs which are not subject to local vote. . . . It is

> becoming increasingly clear that local control cannot in practice be reconciled with the ideals of a democratic society. . . . Local control is a major cause of the dull parochialism and attenuated totalitarianism that characterizes public education in operation.[16]

But because the reaction of white liberals to black people is so mixed with guilt, patronization, and anxiety, the potential force of liberal opposition to what would, under other circumstances, be seen as a sinister movement toward parochialization, is substantially blunted. This often leads to the curious condition of the white liberal who has, with some difficulty, overcome his own parochial roots, and quite explicitly rejected the relevance of his particular past in favor of his participation in a universal future, endorsing black emphasis on African heritage, Swahili, and other forms of black cultural expression.

Our aesthetic and logical sensibilities are, however, only a very minor casualty of a confusing time. Though liberals might be more graceful and Negroes more precise, neither clumsiness nor contradiction is our special concern. The controlling point is that a historic alliance of interest and purpose between white liberals, schooled in Enlightenment doctrines, and Negro leaders, seeking an integrated future, has now come undone, and that its undoing owes largely to a fundamental disagreement over the validity of community as a legitimate pursuit.*

---

* The rejection of "racism" as a total explanation for the hesitation of many liberals to endorse community control, is quite intended. Given the history of white America, some blacks now insist that the burden of proof is on whites—that is, that whites can be assumed to be racists unless they present very persuasive evidence to the contrary. Perhaps such a view is efficient, and, on the whole, safer than its opposite, from an activist's perspective. A student's perspective is bound to be less interested in efficiency and safety than in accuracy; at least so far as liberals are concerned, I see no reason to impute racism where other explanations explain more. "Racism," for example, does not begin to explain the very real anguish many liberals feel these days; the understanding here pursued does. I have no quarrel with those black activists who ignore liberal anguish; that is hardly

Community

The problem of community control as a social theory may now be stated more precisely: traditional liberal assessments of community are incompatible with current black assertions of community. If the incompatibility is to be modified, liberals must either move towards a new understanding or blacks must retreat from their present understanding. We turn now, therefore, to a critical examination of the two positions.

For reasons that have little to do with the racial crisis in the United States, the traditional liberal perspective towards community can be sharply questioned, on at least two different grounds. The first, and more limited question, goes to the issue of whether Enlightenment visions of perfect rationality describe anything now conceivable as even a potential of mankind. For if they do not, it will not do simply to assert that an ideal does not have to be attainable in order to be valuable. There is room, of course, for difference between the actual and the ideal, but, as Walter Lippmann once suggested, an ideal must at the very least describe a plausible reality in order to be useful. If not, it is a false ideal,

> . . . bad . . . in the sense that it is bad for a fat man to try to be a ballet dancer. An ideal should express the true possibilities of its subject. When it does not it perverts the true possibilities. The ideal of the omnicompetent, sovereign citizen is, in my opinion, such a false ideal. It is unattainable. The pursuit of it is misleading.[17]

At the broadest level, the lessons of the twentieth century have clearly shown the anti-community ideal of liberal doctrine to be unattainable. Insofar as that doctrine replaces community, as well as other nonrational bases of association,

---

a problem they can afford to be concerned with. I am, I confess, offended by those white radicals who dismiss the anguish as a hypocritic mask. Inadequacy should never be confused with evil, even though such confusion simplifies analysis. Simple analysis is often wrong analysis, and wrong analysis of a problem is a bad basis for solution.

with a thoroughly rational humanity, we have been witness to a tragically large assortment of countervailing evidence; though this be the century in which man masters space, this is also and ineradicably the century of Auschwitz. Whoever remains invincibly confident of man's ultimate capacity to destroy the beast in man is historically illiterate.

One may, however, conclude that rationality is unlikely, or even impossible, without coming to endorse continuing irrationality, as represented by the organic community or in other, more sinister, ways. Indeed, the more general liberal disposition is to insist that the private loyalties which characterize community are chiefly responsible for man's violence to man. Were universal brotherhood approached, we should all be better off. The fact that men continue to act on their ethnocentric loyalties is what accounts for evil, and, though the future ideal may be remote, the present reality cannot be thought acceptable.

And if it is that reality, a reality clearly far short of universal brotherhood, which is responsible for evil and aggression, then man's obdurate clinging to his group is a fact that must be fought, even though the odds on victory be slight.

Yet, if Lippmann is at all correct, assertion of universal brotherhood as the desired alternative to ethnocentric loyalty may not be the most sensible way of dealing with the negative consequences of ethnocentrism; pursuit of the perfect may impede advent of the good. Indeed, given the accumulation of evidence on the persistence of community, the universal ideal must be seen as utopian, and, therefore, not a meaningful alternative to community. Alternatives, if they are to be taken seriously, are to be plausible, and, in the case at hand, plausibility would suggest an alternative not quite so discrepant from reality as universal brotherhood.

Accordingly, one might suggest as a replacement for universal brotherhood a doctrine, say, of universal cousinhood. An ethic of universal cousinhood, while acknowledging kinship in the family of man, would, presumably, permit people to be selective in their fraternity, a selectivity denied by the ethic of universal brotherhood. It suggests a rather more variegated kinship system than conventional doctrine, thus beginning more nearly from where most people are. Also, it is a more proximate goal, whether or not it is an appropriate terminal.

But if a more modest statement of purpose is to replace the unattainable present ideal, a serious empirical question is raised. We do not know whether it is possible for men to feel special affinity towards some without coming to feel hostile to all others. That is, we do not know whether men can simultaneously be committed as brothers and sensitive as cousins. There is at least some reason to suppose that a proper regard for mankind in general is not compatible with a special regard for groups less than the whole.

We may put this problem rather differently. There is a near-perfect literary statement of it in *The Merchant of Venice*. When Shylock pleads his case, he stresses his common humanity with his tormentors:

> Hath not a Jew eyes? Hath not a Jew hands, organs, dimensions, senses, affections, passions? Fed with the same food, subject to the same diseases, healed by the same means, warmed and cooled by the same winter and summer as a Christian is? If you prick us, do we not bleed? If you tickle us, do we not laugh? If you poison us, do we not die?

These are familiar phrases, and suggest quite nicely the conventional liberal understanding. That which sets us apart, one from the other, is superficial; in the things that matter, we are the same. There is, however, a point at which Antonio invites Shylock to dinner. Shylock, who observes the Jewish dietary laws, responds as follows: "I will walk with you, talk with you, buy with you, sell with you, and so following; but I will not eat with you, drink with you, or pray with you."

The empirical question is precisely this: is it possible to refuse to eat, drink, and pray with your neighbor and still to expect to walk, talk, buy, and sell with him? (The obverse question is also interesting, and we shall come to it anon: is it possible to walk, talk, buy, and sell with your neighbor without coming to eat, drink, and pray with him?)

The issue may now be formally stated. Cultural pluralism suggests a society in which diversity is legitimate. All too often, however, random diversity has been equated with cultural pluralism. Let us, instead, define the relationships of groups within any society according to two variables: cohesion and interaction. Cohesion is a measure of the internal strength of the group, the degree to which its members depend upon each other. Interaction is a measure of association of members of one group with members of other groups. Now, groups may be more or less cohesive, and more or less interactive. A society marked by high group cohesion and low group interaction is a caste society. A society marked by low group cohesion and high interaction is a mass society. A society marked by high cohesion and high interaction is a pluralistic society. (The fourth case, low cohesion and low interaction may be represented in transitional societies where the old ties have been subverted, but interaction is not yet significant.)

Whether a plural society is empirically plausible is an open question. But it does constitute an alternative to a radically universalist society, in which cohesion is illegitimate. Since I take the question of whether a society based on affective universal brotherhood to be a closed question—such a society is not plausible—I conclude that what must be implied, empirically, by insistence on universalism is, in fact, low cohesion (groups being illegitimate) and high interaction. And that is mass society.

Thus, liberal social critics, reacting against societies composed largely of ethnic enclaves and exclusive fraternities, demanded that the barriers be torn down. In so doing, however, they have generated their other bête noire, the mass society, with all its anonymity, indifference, rootlessness. The error, evidently, was to attack the structural aspect—the existence of groups—rather than to attack the characteristic relationship among groups.

Converting lonely crowds into meaningful entities, given people's evident predispositions, requires acceptance of man's differential capacity for loyalty. The fact that men feel closer to some than to others might, in this respect, be viewed as a resource rather than as a threat.

How is it possible that those same observers who have sought more secular orientations and more impersonal rules have simultaneously sought universal brotherhood? A world of brothers seems, at first blush, substantially more affective than a rational, achievement-oriented world. Our commitments to brothers, after all, are based on ascription, that is, on their being our brothers, and not, say, on achievement. And this would seem to violate the rational ideal, the very definition of modernity.

The two are not, however, so discrepant. For in a world in which all men are brothers, brotherhood means something very different from what is usually intended by the word. It is, obviously, a substantially diluted relationship. Even discounting for the obvious symbolism of the concept, the most that one can imagine is a rather more empathic world than ours. It is not a world of significant affect, and certainly not of equal affect to all. Indeed, thus far, at least, if the doctrine of universal brotherhood has had any issue at all, it has been sibling rivalry rather than brotherly love.

In short, the second ground for challenging the traditional liberal perspective is not that it is unattainable, but that the pursuit of its attainment necessarily leads to a condition little better than the condition it seeks to repair.

Fear of the destabilizing consequences of mass society, from personal anomie to political demagoguery, and, ultimately, totalitarianism, has been a favored subject of intellectual disquisition among those same critics who have also adhered to Enlightenment doctrines. Where the inconsistency has been recognized—where, that is, it has been clear that ideological prohibition on group identification necessarily created the conditions of mass society—the antidote most commonly prescribed has been replacement of organic community by contractual community. Among political scientists, for example, much has been made of the importance of interest groups and political parties as stabilizing loyalties. These groups are clearly instrumental rather than expressive, and where their membership has used them for expressive purposes they have been frowned upon by those committed to rationalism. City planners have been much concerned with the concept of the neighborhood, but their traditional commitments have, on the whole, led them to insist that neighborhoods be inhabited by essentially randomly selected people. The proper basis of association and identification, in this view, is the neighborhood itself, the shared instrumental interests which neighbors have with each other rather than any prior loyalties that each has brought with him. Thus the faceless city is replaced with the faceless neighborhood, where neighbors are recognized for what they are worth, rather than for who they are.

American cities are dotted with successful examples of neighborhoods based on shared interest and taste, but they are almost always in the area of universities or are highly specialized places, such as Greenwich Village, which cater to idiosyncratic clienteles. The university experience offers no basis for generalization, since the university is, in its own way, an organic rather than an artificial community, and is, in any case, highly restricted to those who have been graced with the liberal dispensation. Indeed, we may speculate that university people, who are the leading opponents of conventional organic communities, both seek to generalize from their own social position, which they perceive as beyond community, and fail to appreciate the degree to which they, too, have fraternal requirements that are not wholly rational.

Most Americans, it appears, prefer to make their friendship choices not on the basis of shared interest so much as on the basis of shared roots. Perhaps this is because they suppose that interests are less durable than roots. To live with people "like oneself" continues to mean, for most of us, to live with people of the same race, religion, and/or ethnic background.

While such bases of selection are declining, especially among the college-educated, it is not clear whether we ought to be more impressed with the decline, hastened, as it has been, by an ideology militantly opposed to such parochialisms, or with the much slower rate of decline, despite the ideological encouragement, than we had expected about the turn of the century. The fact that the college educated are quicker to discard the past cannot be taken as evidence that with enlightenment comes liberation. It may just as well be evidence that colleges, whether explicitly or implicitly, in accordance with their controlling ideological perspectives, hold community up to ridicule. Social scientists are, and need to be, taught to step outside the boundaries of their own past, in order to achieve social scientific perspective. Yet professional perspective may easily be read as civic ideology; social science may come to be seen not as a tool, but as a way of life.

In any event, if what replaces community, whether it is destroyed by technology, or ideology, or mobility, is loneliness rather than liberty, then the value of the universalist perspective may be challenged.

Negroes as a Community

In effect, the assertion of community by blacks may be read in part as follows:

> Our chief mentors in the battle for civil rights were upper middle class liberals, who, for reasons of their own, cling to a vision of a universalistic social order. We accepted their belief and their doctrine, and acted upon it. It produced some rewards, but, in the end, we found ourselves still unmelted in the hypothetical pot. And, in looking about more carefully, we have found that other groups have retained their particular identities, have resisted wholesale assimilation. We conclude, therefore, that liberals are trying to impose upon us a standard which derives from their philosophical ideal rather than from the sweaty facts of American social life. We rather suspect, in fact, that liberals have mis-

read the American social experience, for they are, in
their own way, too far removed from its major elements.
Moreover, we are interested in tactics, not in utopias.
We shall, therefore, resist being held to a form of behavior which we find both non-productive and outside
the mainstream of American life, which is still in its
core, and despite liberal wishes, group life. We shall
resist being the guinea-pigs for a vision of society so
out of touch with social reality.

Black power and black pride and black community are
concepts which took most liberals by surprise. Not only did
they violate the central understanding of the liberal-Negro
alliance, but they asserted an identity most white liberals had
simply not recognized. Even sensitive and honorable men had
not imagined that being black in America might have rewards
as well as penalties. So, for example, Thomas Pettigrew,
noting that Indians, Chinese, and Japanese "all had proud
cultures of their own, which were for a long time reasonably
well-maintained in America," goes on to observe that

Negroes in America were never so fortunate. Though
possessing proud cultures of their own, African slaves
brought to North America were systematically stripped
of their cultural heritage. . . . Negroes have therefore
never been in the position of the culturally insulated
Indians, Chinese, or Japanese in America, and arguments about the beneficial features of such insulation
for them are neither realistic nor relevant. . . . Negroes
are hopelessly identified with American culture, a fact
which translates separation into oppression rather than
comfort.[18]

It is possible that sentiments such as these express an
earlier reality more accurately than they describe the present
disposition of black Americans. Alternatively, it may be that
white understandings have been broadened in recent years,
so that there is now a growing appreciation of the authenticity of a black culture which has been with us all along, but
which most were unable to accept as recently as a decade

ago. Whichever the more accurate statement, surely one reason that white liberals have traditionally believed that color should be treated as irrelevant has been their belief that color is, in fact, irrelevant. White liberals have not, for the most part, conceived that Negroes could be tied to one another by anything save their common persecution. There has been, therefore, no need to invoke the pluralist ethic with respect to Negroes, for Negroes have not been generally recognized—again, until very recently—as a potential group.

I do not believe it seemly for aliens to a culture to debate whether or not the culture is "valid." If people believe it to be valid for themselves, then it is valid. Whether black power is an assertion of a durable subculture in American society, or is simply a tactical way station, on the road to ultimate integration, is not, at the moment, of central importance. But it may be worth noting that the history of the past fifteen years or so has provided the black community with many of the central features of viable cultures—heroes, place-names, songs, proud memories. Thus, even if those who presume to weigh such matters conclude that Negro American history is not an authentic basis for cultural assertion are, in some sense, correct, even if studying Swahili is a diversion and caring about Africa a snare, even if the role of blacks in America's development was trivial, even if slavery is best forgotten, more recent experience cannot be discounted. That history, at the very least, has caused the shared stigma of blackness to be seen as a badge of honor. So, even if the expression of the new allegiance is, in its origins, primarily a reaction-formation, its authenticity grows with each passing day. For with each day, the myth and mystique of blackness is elaborated, amplified, made more potent, and hence more viable.

The more interesting question that is raised asks whether a community can be created which will avoid the dreary fate of ethnocentrism, that is, whether legitimation of community assertiveness by blacks will not simply add to the social burden of intergroup hostility, whether it will not again postpone the era of liberation from myth.

Blacks are understandably impatient with such a question, for to ask of them that they bypass the common condition is to invoke, once again, a double standard in which white groups are accepted, however reluctantly, as realities, while black people are held to a far "higher" standard. But black impatience does not in itself make the question unimportant; it merely suggests some constraints on the answer. Observers are still entitled, and even required, to ask whether a black community in the making can be more attractive, which is to say, less ethnocentric, than other communities have been. Since the white liberals who ask such a question have, over the years, compiled a fairly active record in opposing the malfeasance of organic groups in white society, the issue is less the invocation of a double standard than the desire to learn from the past, to avoid compounding the social problem.

In short: is it possible to imagine a black community which conforms to the model of the plural society rather than to the model of the caste society? Or, returning to earlier imagery, is it possible that black people can fashion a brotherhood that will not view all non-brothers as enemies, but rather as cousins?

That there is a brotherhood on the way is clear, as even the language now suggests. It is not trivial that black people today have taken the religious tradition of calling each other "brother" and "sister" into the secular arena. It is also clear that one aspect of the new brotherhood is an increase in expressive hostility to non-brothers, that is, to white people. Whether there has been an increase in felt hostility, or, as seems equally likely, an increase in the confidence and social support which permits the expression of long-felt hostility, is not clear. It may be that some such hostility is necessary in order to generate the desired cohesion; "inness" often becomes more meaningful when contrasted to "outness." Yet it is possible that the explicit hostility which appears functional in the embryonic stages of developing a new allegiance is superfluous as that cohesion produces its own experience to draw upon. People may come together as a group because others treat them as a group, but once drawn together, it is not only their treatment by others that keeps them together, but also the things they do together.

Accordingly, it is important that the things they do together not be limited to things done with respect to outsiders. So long as the only basis of association is instrumental, hostility can be expected to grow. It is only through the encouragement and endorsement of organic development that more creative communion can be realized. Thus, even though "others" may, for whatever reason, suspect the authenticity of black community, supposing it to be entirely a reaction to discrimination, and even though the traditional ethic prefers instrumental to organic association, the capacity of the black community to enter into a pluralistic relationship with other American groups depends on support for its internal and particularistic development. The alternatives are an unstable alliance, lacking in cohesion and hence in structure, drawn together only in anger, or a highly cohesive, but fundamentally ethnocentric, isolated—hence insulated—community.

Organic development of the black community will not, in itself, assure entrance into the plural mold. Two other elements are required as well, both more the responsibility of whites than of blacks. There is, first, the issue of our public rhetoric. For reasons that can be variously explained, a significant segment of the liberal elite has taken to endorsing the most outrageous descriptions of our current state. Orgiastic confessions of collective guilt have overshadowed serious efforts at reformation. In particular, we have taken to identifying our problems in terms which make their solution impossible. So, for example, the term "racism." If, as some have claimed, this country and its people are fundamentally racist, then the situation may well be irretrievable. Insofar as those who employ the term and other

equally imprecise descriptions of our condition have a working model for change, they must be thinking that significant
reform depends upon total honesty; whites are redeemable
only after they have publicly confessed their sins.

The notion of redemption through confession is venerable.
Yet in the political sector not less than in the religious, the
risk we run by relying on that notion is that confession, far
from being the first step towards reformation, is a replacement for it. This is particularly true in cases where the sins
we confess are ill-defined. The more severe the chastisement,
the happier the chastised; confession itself becomes the pur-
gative.

It is far easier to beat the breast than to reform, so the
instrumental importance of the confession is not surprising.
But in the end, both the critics who pursue reform and their
audience of sinners are engaging in ritual behavior except
when they specify how the lamented evils may be operationally defined and, hence, programmatically addressed.
Until, for example, we are able to describe the respects in
which an alleged racist is engaging in racist behavior, and to
distinguish among degrees of racism, the term will continue
to reflect a failure of intellect, a rejection of analysis in favor
of ritual.

It is a failure with serious negative potential. We can
surmise that the Kerner Commission sought to shock a slum-
bering nation into consciousness. But the use of rhetorical
overkill is as likely to persuade people that a situation is
beyond repair as it is to spur them to new action, especially
if the needed action is nowhere described. Moreover, expression by some whites of the most sweeping and vulgar
indictments of white society supports the latent tendency in
the black community to turn its back on all interaction with
whites. It supports and encourages the development of a
black consciousness which is essentially reactive, rather than
authentic. Since the reactive impulse is already intense, the
challenge of the moment is not how to enlarge it, but how
to create the conditions for a black community that is more

balanced between cohesion and interaction than other ethnic communities have tended to be. Ideally, the plural structure calls for communities which are parochial in structure but universal in content. Intensification of an already staggering tradition of hostility encourages only the parochialism; it supports black community cohesion, but inhibits interaction.

It is sometimes argued that the black community must become still more cohesive before it engages in interaction, lest the interaction be from weakness rather than strength, and hence destructive of community. Our social sensors are not so delicate that we can know precisely when the threshold of community consciousness has been reached, and structured interaction can proceed without serious threat to that consciousness. But that is a problem only if the interaction proposed is based on old models which stress individual interchange. At some point—and we have either recently reached that point, or are very close to it—it becomes possible to interact with individuals-as-members-of-groups; when that point is reached, and if the ideology is open to such interaction, persistence of accusatory rhetoric becomes a dangerous anachronism.

To suggest that a shift in rhetoric will, of itself, make interaction more likely is at best an oversimplification. For the grievances to which the rhetoric alludes are real, not fancied, and the hostilities it supports are rooted in history, not oratory. In order to generate productive intercommunal interaction, the facts of white malfeasance towards blacks must change, as well as the words which distort those facts. This is hardly a novel assertion; it is what liberals, and responsible conservatives, have been saying for decades. The novelty, if novelty there be, lies in the identification of one of the facts that needs changing as the fact of liberal, individually-oriented ideology itself. So long as we continue to rely exclusively upon a model which calls for the assimilation of Negroes into the dominant society—so long, that is, as we deny the relevance of color—so long will we subvert a cohesion which is increasingly a fact of Negro American life in favor of an ideology which has never been especially persuasive.

Woodrow Wilson once said that "There are no minorities in the United States. There are no national minorities, racial minorities, or religious minorities. The whole concept and basis of the United States precludes them." In so saying, he articulated the basic liberal premise. That premise is at best an arguable description of the facts of American social life; it is, as a statement of purpose, no more convincing. It has been rejected, finally, by black people themselves, at least for the time being, and whites who would address the issue of race relations fruitfully might therefore turn away from their fixation with Enlightenment prescriptions towards the more reality-oriented concern for group life in America.

The choice of words here is important. The new black cohesiveness is taken, in some quarters, to imply a desire for separatism, and the implication is sustained by some black leaders. Separatism, however, is no more creative a model than atomistic integration. Moreover, it offers too comforting a cover to those who do not accept equality. Blackness may, indeed, be relevant, but it is not all that is relevant. The normative task is to create a situation in which meaningful choices are available, neither insisting on integration nor closed to community. Whites who would specify how Negroes must come to terms with white society are arrogant; they retain their traditional position as guardians of the gate. It is choice that is wanted, not the imposition of one utopian model or another. And choice requires the removal of external constraint.

Public policy, then, cannot demand that Negroes be dispersed; it must provide the option of dispersal. Public policy cannot invest only in communities rather than individuals; it must, however, accept the legitimacy of community, as an option.

In the end, it is still not certain that the pluralistic model is attainable. Its viability depends upon people's capacity to live with structured tension and ambiguity. But neither the exclusive preoccupation with interaction, which has been the white liberal mode, nor the fixation on cohesion, which is increasingly the black militant mode, seems a happy alternative. Movement towards the assertion of community by blacks is less a sign of failure of the system than a sign of weakness in the theory; hence it is the theory, in the first instance, which needs revision, and the system only insofar as it is based upon the theory. Community control as a social theory is, then, not so much a revolutionary departure as it is the latest chapter in a debate that has gone on for many years.

CHAPTER THREE

COMMUNITY CONTROL AND POLITICAL THEORY

I F THE CONCEPT and status of community in American thought are ambiguous, the meaning of "control" is hardly less so, especially in the area of education. The system ostensibly endorses widespread lay participation in framing educational policies, but is less certain in its judgment regarding actual control of those policies. To the traditional question "Who shall judge?" the earlier simplistic answer "the people shall judge" now seems hopelessly inadequate. Which people? Those with special competence or people in general? Those who choose to participate actively, or all the people? And if all the people, what shall be the mechanisms for expressing their judgment? How shall dissenting judgments be accounted for? How can we insure that the executors of their judgment are faithful to their intent? The questions are endless, the answers complex. The only thing that can be said with reasonable certainty is that it will simply not do to assert that "the people" should "govern" themselves; however appealing the sentiment, it provides very little guidance. We are, therefore, required to examine more closely the ambiguities of "control."

Professionalism and Participation

The prevailing belief, assiduously fostered by schoolmen, has been that education is a professional enterprise, and, accordingly, its management (i.e., control) is to be left to experts. The ultimate justification for democratic decision-making procedures is the assumption that political truth is fallible; if it were possible to articulate infallible truth, then, presumably, we would entrust our destiny to those who possess it—if we knew, and could agree on, who they are. Since expertise suggests, if not infallibility, at least a far superior wisdom, those who can lay plausible claim to the title "expert" commonly view themselves as exempt from the requirements of democracy. We do not vote on what kind of fuel cell to use aboard our missiles, since we assume that that is a matter which men with special training are best qualified to judge. The role of the public, in theory, is to decide whether there shall be missiles at all—that is, to determine broad policy directions for society.

But in turning to the field of education, it is difficult to know what is policy, what is technique. As Thomas H. Eliot pointed out more than a decade ago, professional educators believe deeply that the critical areas of personnel (except for the school superintendent) and curriculum are properly areas for expert judgment, and they have countered efforts by lay people to encroach on the experts.[1] In the main, public control over the schools, insofar as it is expressed through school boards, has been limited to very general policy direction. Indeed, a recent study suggests that school boards often act as agencies of legitimation for the educational professionals, rather than as representatives of the community to the school administration.[2] Other studies suggest that school boards in large cities are typically preoccupied with political issues, and especially with those issues arising from the problem of racial integration, rather than with such central educational issues as what gets taught, and how.[3] The appropriate conclusion, therefore, would appear to be that the traditional mythology of popular control over American education, via appointed or elected lay boards, substantially distorts the reality of school politics.

This should not come as a surprise. In many areas of

public life (as in private life), there is a serious discrepancy between ideology and behavior. It is only when our attention is called to the discrepancy that we are urged to reconcile the two, either by changing our behavior or by reframing our ideology.

Nor is it only belief and behavior that diverge; we even manage, quite comfortably, for the most part, to sustain quite discrepant beliefs. Thus, for example, while the popular mythology holds that public schools are popularly controlled, a stirring reflection of grass roots democracy at its best, most evidence indicates that parents prefer to leave educational matters to professional educators. It is only lately, largely as a result of matters having to do with race, that the contradictions in our belief system, and between our beliefs and our behaviors, have become so apparent. That we could at one and the same time endorse the myth of participation, which shades into public control, and the myth of expertise, which shades into professional control, suggests a decided ambiguity in our myth system, an ambiguity which finds a close parallel in the reflections of scholars on the meaning and purposes of American democracy.

It is, of course, perfectly plain that the American polity falls far short of classical statements of democratic theory. Our citizens are neither so well-informed, nor so interested, nor so active, as the more idyllic statements of early democratic theorists proposed they should be, or would be. Interest groups of all sorts, political parties, specialized and secret information, advertising—all these and more have had to be accounted for in restatements of the meaning of contemporary democracy. The most serious discrepancy between classical theory and contemporary reality has been with respect to the question of participation in the political process. Normative democratic theory had emphasized the importance of widespread political participation both as a way of arriving at genuinely dispassionate policies and as a way of producing an enlightened citizenry. Upon observing, however, that significant numbers of citizens failed to participate in even the most rudimentary expressions of political interest, such as elections, democratic theorists were compelled to rethink the original statement. What emerged as the dominant view, until very recently, was a restatement which held that high levels of participation were not, after all, required by the theory; in fact, dramatic increases in participation might well by symptoms of democratic malfunction. While such a view has been put forward by a large number of scholars, its most explicit formulation is by Bernard Berelson, commenting on the paradox that "Individual voters . . . seem unable to satisfy the requirements for a democratic system of government outlined by political theorists (while) the system of democracy does meet certain requirements for a going political organization."[4] How can it be, Berelson asks, that the system appears to work, while its component parts do not? His answer, generally, is that the system cannot tolerate a homogeneous electorate, but requires instead a distribution of qualities; specifically, "we need some people who are active in a certain respect, others in the middle, and still others passive."[5] Apathy cannot only be tolerated, but, so long as it is not without limit, has positive consequences for the democratic polity.[6]

This position and others of kindred perspective have been further elaborated in the work of the democratic pluralists whose central argument has been that democracy can flourish even when limited numbers of people participate in political life, so long as among those who do participate there is disagreement, and, therefore, competition.

In recent years, however, the views of the pluralists have come under widespread attack. Some critics have alleged that there is, in fact, little competition among the participant elites; others have emphasized the potential benefits of participation, which are denied to large numbers of people in a system accustomed to leaving decision-making to a small group; still others have been most concerned with the ideological bias of a system in which a disproportionate number of the nonparticipants are poor. In general, it is this last consideration which has provided the most powerful incentive to the critics of democratic revisionism. The early work of C. Wright Mills was largely ignored, or attacked, by most scholars until poverty was "discovered" in America.[7] Up to that time, it was difficult, apparently, to become very exercised about the pre-eminence of middle class values in American public policy. After all, America was essentially a middle class country. But when, during the 1960's, it became dramatically clear that a minority of Americans numbering in the tens-of-millions was not, by any stretch of the imagination, middle class, the problem of bias could not be so simply dismissed. Indeed, it could be—and was—argued that the belated attention given the problem of poverty was itself proof that a system which did not encourage the participation of all elements was likely to ignore the interests of the nonparticipants. And, since nonparticipation was not randomly distributed, but occurred most commonly among members of a (relatively) discrete social class, that class had to be specifically mobilized for political participation. Otherwise, of course, its interests, now shown clearly to be distinguishable from the interests of other groups, would continue to be ignored.

Yet, though scholarly sentiment regarding general political participation has shifted of late, it would be mistaken to suppose that the ambiguity has been significantly reduced, much less eliminated. We are still not certain—that is, there is still no general consensus—how much a democratic system, in a complex economy, must be based on popular participation, how much an expert judgment.

If this ambiguity is apparent in the general political system, how much more marked it is in those subsystems of the polity which claim exemption from normal democratic requirements. Among the managers of public institutions, popular participation is, typically, viewed as an annoyance. A civil servant is inclined to view himself as a technical administrator; if he were not, what justification would there be for civil service examinations, or for the concept of professional merit? And, if the task is defined as one which involves specialized competence, on what basis can lay participation—i.e., amateurism—be justified? In general, the more concerned a group is with underscoring its status as a profession, and the more plausible its claim to professional status, the more likely it is to assert that it deserves immunity from popular participation.

Although teaching school was not, in the early years of public education, viewed as a profession (and some critics of public education continue to argue that it has not become more a profession since), educators have eagerly sought, and, in the main, achieved, professional status during this century. While it is not entirely clear what the concept of "profession" depends upon, certain formal criteria are satisfied by the field of education. Most important, perhaps, is that professional graduate schools of education exist, quite apart from what they teach and whether what they teach is significant. Any field which can point to the existence of special courses of advanced training leading to special degrees can plausibly assert that its practitioners are pursuing a profession, rather than merely a vocation. Thus, as Lawrence Cremin notes, Dean Russell of Teachers College at Columbia University "never ceased to point out that the College was the 'professional school of Columbia University for the advanced professional training of teachers' and that its place in the university system was 'analogous to that of the schools of Law, Medicine, and Applied Science.' "[8] In short, educators themselves insist that they are professionals; their status as professionals, in turn, provides one major justification for their insulation from the normal political process.

At the same time, however, both teachers and laymen continued to stress the virtues of public control of education. Thus, James E. Allen, then New York State Commissioner of Education (later United States Commissioner of Education): "The preservation and enhancement of local control must be a special concern of our leadership."[9] Local control, Allen argues, provides the following benefits: healthy diver-

sity, flexibility, ferment and experimentation, imaginative
approaches to school problems, and grass roots interest in
education.[10]

The difficulty, of course, is in reconciling the competing
implications of expertise and public control. For if the educators can convince the public that what they are involved
in is a field which depends for its proper pursuit upon specialized training, on what basis can lay people contend with
the professionals?

Against which, again, it may be argued that educators are
specialists in technique, but only the public can properly take
responsibility for defining the aims of education. Such an
argument, however, has at least two problematic aspects.

First, as we have noted, it is difficult, if not impossible, to
determine where substance ends and technique begins. This
is particularly true if we accept those theories of education
which hold that the technique has direct and central substantive implications. Such theories, whether derived from
John Dewey or from Edgar Friedenberg, explicitly deny that
method and purpose can be divorced. On the contrary, the
method reflects, sustains, logically implies, the purpose—or
subverts it. Similarly, a whole series of school-related issues
cannot be clearly identified as entirely technical or wholly
ideological. To which category, for example, do school construction and school architecture belong? Although super-
ficially a technical question, the physical design of the school
immediately implies substantive educational choices, as hundreds of American communities engaged in debating the
merits of "flexible schools" are now learning.

Second, even if it were possible to mark a clear boundary
between ends and means in education, if we conclude that
the public shall be restricted to debating those matters which
come under the heading of "ends," we open the system to an
unnerving kind of debate. We encourage citizens to participate in school politics, in order to put empirical flesh onto
the theoretical bones of public control (many citizens respond, if for no other reason than that schools typically

represent the single largest investment of local communities, and, therefore, have the strongest impact on tax rates), and then we prohibit these same citizens from debating "mundane" issues, insisting, instead, that they restrict themselves to debating fundamental purposes and ideologies. The result, as Robert Wood has noted, is a kind of perpetual constitutional convention, a politics of ideology without parallel anywhere else in the political system.[11]

The tension between the competing claims of expertise and participation cannot so easily be resolved. There is no simple formula—though, like the Holy Grail, the formula is endlessly pursued—which will do. Yet without a formula, without some general standard to which school boards and professionals in dispute can appeal, how are we to render unto the board that which is the board's, and unto the professionals that which is theirs?

The difficulty in arriving at a persuasive theoretical answer to this question has been illustrated in countless episodes in American educational history, of which the best known is probably the Scopes trial. To mention the Scopes trial in this context is to run the risk of the reader immediately concluding that the issue is not, after all, so complex. Was not the ban on teaching Darwinian theory a direct challenge to everything education stands for? And, if so, how does the Scopes case illustrate the theme of ambiguity?

Yet what are we to make of Darrow's assertion, in the course of his examination of Bryan, that "We have the purpose of preventing bigots and ignoramuses from controlling the education of the United States"? Does not the doctrine of public control rest, finally, upon the indisputable right of bigots and ignoramuses, as well as others, to involve themselves in providing guidelines for public education? And, if to involve themselves, also, if they be in a majority, to control? The system, after all, allows for that. The most definitive act of school boards across the land is the selection of a superintendent. There is no external control over the selection; a board can, if it will, choose a mountebank as readily as a respected educator. It can assert virtually whatever criteria it chooses in making its selection; indeed, where it is proscribed from using race, age, or sex as criteria, it is left chiefly with political and ideological criteria. It can search for Americanists, or evolutionists, as astrologers, or anything else that it wishes.

The theoretical question at issue here has to do with the purposes of public education. There is no serious quarrel that one of those purposes is to transmit the values of the adult community to the younger generation. Even the most caustic critics of those values, those who most emphasize the liberating function of education, who most pursue a spirit of free inquiry, do not dispute that the community, as the sponsor of education, is also entitled, in some measure, to provide for its own maintenance through the educational system. The rub is in the limitation "in some measure." For what if the values the community seeks to transmit be narrow? What if they be at variance with the values of other, and neighboring communities, or with communities more broadly defined, such as the states, or the nation itself? If the citizens of any local community view certain doctrines as pernicious, and certain teachings as inimical to their own purposes, are they to be prevented from pointing the system away from such doctrines and such teachings? If they are so prevented, what is left of "grass roots" democracy?

Because the schools deal so explicitly with values, expertise cannot be restricted to technical competence alone. There is, in fact, no way of sharply delineating the boundaries that separate laymen and professionals, since almost every substantive educational decision both derives from, and points to, a value stance, and since almost every policy decision has direct, and comprehensive, implications for technique.

Nonetheless, the local community is not the only community of concern; its value commitments are not binding on other communities, nor is it permitted complete autonomy in giving expression to those commitments. Thus, for example, the nation has proclaimed its own interest in racial integration, and because the national interest prevails over the local when the two are in conflict, local exceptions are no longer—at least in theory—permitted. (Yet the nation does not proscribe the teaching of white supremacy in the classroom.)

The nation has been reluctant to intervene in most matters, preferring to leave to the local community as much autonomy over the education of "its own" children as it possibly could. As a result, the professionals and the community must develop their own framework for relationship, community by community, in each of the thousands of school districts of the United States. It would be utterly intolerable to raise, in each case, and repeatedly, the kinds of underlying questions we have referred to. No community could long survive the debate which would ensue. Even though attacks on school professionals have often served as vehicles for political mobility by politicians, disruptive tension appears to affect most communities only some of the time, with perhaps some communities being affected most of the time. As to the rest, there has emerged, in the typical American way, a working arrangement which comes nowhere near satisfying the requirement of theoretical neatness, but which does provide a satisfactory modus vivendi—which is all most communities ask for.

The central feature of that arrangement is the acceptance by school boards that their basic function is to present the needs of the schools, as defined by the professionals, to the general public. A related task involves the exercise of fiscal control over the professionals, a way of asserting the public's financial (but not ideological) interest in the schools. Hence, much of the debate which occupies the time of school boards has to do with educational "frills." Some of these frills are very closely related to educational ideologies, but they are more commonly argued in terms of costs, since the terms of the argument are then more familiar and the passions are more tempered.

Failing all else, the professionals can always try to define an issue as strictly technical, and hence outside the scope of lay authority. Thus, for example, a school board angered over the periodicals to which a local high school library subscribes, on the grounds that their content violates the values of the community, might well encounter a response by the professionals that the guidelines published by the (professional) School Librarian's Association include recommendations on acquisition, recommendations, needless to say, put forward by specialists, and hence beyond debate by laymen. Only a courageous or impassioned few would have the audacity to pit themselves against credentialed majesty.

The working arrangement between experts and citizens serves to keep the social peace. But there are problems that gnaw through the arrangement and finally erupt into major disputes. In such disputes, liberals have, for the most part, sided with the professionals against the lay people.

At first glance, this may seem somewhat curious, since grass roots participation has long been a hallowed tenet of the liberal platform. But there are two powerful circumstances which account for the apparent contradiction. First, and most generally, liberal tendencies have traditionally been rather elitist, the platform acknowledgment of the virtues of participation notwithstanding.

The small town and town meeting have never been the liberal's special metier, for "the people" are likely to be know-nothings, unenlightened, brutish. Comfort to the people, yes; power to the people, no.

More specifically, and as if in confirmation of the liberal suspicion of participation, disputes over who shall control the schools have tended, especially during the middle third of this century, to pit conservative laymen against more liberal professionals. It was Dwight Eisenhower, in the 1950's, who emerged as the leading champion of continued local control, arguing that federal aid to education would be "another vehicle by which believers in paternalism, if not outright socialism, will gain still additional power for the central government."[12] More important, support for local control, during the 1950's, implied support for opposition to the United Nations, to sex education, to racial integration, to progressive education generally, for these were the issues around which citizens organized to participate in school management. To endorse localism would mean, in context, to endorse the extreme parochialism which substitutes for wisdom (as liberals define wisdom) in thousands of communities.

Yet it would be too much to say that liberals have energetically sought to substitute state or federal control for local control. Some have, but most have recognized that in their own suburban communities, the assertion of local control makes possible an enlightened and progressive educational system. While movement towards larger and more heterogeneous districts would clearly help to de-parochialize traditional systems, it would also, and inevitably, limit the autonomy of those who perceive themselves as the liberated. Thus we find, for example, that despite all the liberal tongue-clacking at the backwardness of the Boston school system, any suggestion that the schools of Brookline, or Newton, or Lexington, be merged with those of Boston, is greeted by the enlightened residents of these suburban communities with icy hostility.

Instead of pursuing a removal of local control to a higher level of government, or a substantial enlargement of present school districts, liberals have tended to place their bets on an enlargement of the authority of the professionals. This strategy is particularly appealing in smaller and more affluent suburbs. In large cities, where the electorate is more heterogeneous, and the pressures on school boards therefore more diverse, it is less popular. There, the professional frequently emerges as an embattled bureaucrat, using his credentials to defend his organization, trying desperately to maintain a balance between working class constituents and liberal activists.[13] But where the liberal ideology holds sway, support for professionals is the norm, and is easily justified as accordant with the perquisites of specialized competence, an extension of the concept of the merit system.

In short: insofar as the question of participation is viewed theoretically, it suffers from the same theoretical ambiguity characteristic of the political system as a whole. And insofar as it is viewed as an empirical question, there is serious doubt as to whether local control means quite what its spokesmen have claimed; instead, a working compromise, the balance tipped in favor of professionals and against citizen participation, is the norm, with a significant variance which derives mainly from the character of the local community.

Legitimacy and Effectiveness

The tension between expertise and participation is closely related to a pair of concepts often used by political scientists to assess the character of political systems: effectiveness and legitimacy. "Effectiveness" speaks to the output of an institution, or, more specifically, to the degree to which consumers are satisfied that it is doing the job they want done. "Legitimacy" is a rather more slippery concept; broadly, it may be taken to refer to the agreement by members of a group (or polity) that those who govern do so rightfully. In general, when a system is viewed as legitimate, those who govern may make many serious errors before people will begin to question the system itself. Their prior disposition will be to condemn the incumbent governors. Only as it becomes clear that no incumbents can do well under the constitutional ordering will the rules themselves be questioned. Similarly, when a system works well, or is effective, even though it may have been initially condemned as illegitimate, it tends, over time, to increase its claim to rightness, thereby earning, as it were, more scope for error. There is, then, a very powerful association between effectiveness and legitimacy.[14]

We usually depend upon experts to produce effective results. So long as the experts succeed, most people are not inclined to question the moral basis of their claim to power. When, however, the experts are ineffective, questions regarding their right to continue in power are to be expected. In democratic systems, the right to power derives from popular election. The only legitimate source of power in a democracy —however power may later be allocated—is the ballot box. This does not mean that all those who govern the institutions of a free society must run for office; it does mean that the governors have either been themselves elected, or were appointed by elected officials. Citizen participation in the choice of governors is the source of governmental legitimacy.

Until recently, most Americans have had little reason to question either the legitimacy or the effectiveness of political arrangements in this country. On the whole, the "rightness" of the system, enshrined in document and holiday, preached in pulpit and in classroom, was supported by, and in turn supported, its perceived effectiveness. The Great Depression was the last great crisis before the present time, but, as it was fundamentally a crisis in effectiveness, the renewed productivity which brought the Depression to an end also brought the modest challenge to systemic legitimacy to an end.

Today, of course, we are in the midst of a far more profound crisis. The apparent incapacity of the political system to deal effectively with a whole range of problems has raised serious questions about the nature of American political arrangements. The public schools, as one agency of the political system, are objects of the general malaise. Moreover, they are especially vulnerable to attack, on several counts.

There is a long history of criticism in the area of public education in this country. But, until recently, almost all of the criticism was directed against the job the schools were doing, or failing to do—i.e., against the alleged ineffectiveness of the schools. As we have suggested, prolonged dissatisfaction with performance leads easily to questions regarding legitimacy. This is particularly so where, as in the case of the schools, ineffectiveness is not only prolonged, but also where a specific clientele is its victim, and where ameliorative efforts make no discernible difference. For when these conditions prevail, there is no significant prospect that the system will undergo dramatic improvement. Failing such improvement, the critics can only conclude that either (a) the job cannot be done at all, or (b) the job cannot be done under prevailing arrangements.

Note, however, that the roots of the crisis in legitimacy are fed by the crisis in effectiveness. Were they not so fed, we might still encounter demands for a reordering of the educational system, but it is difficult to imagine that such demands would generate much popular enthusiasm. In other words, even if the system were, as its critics and their supporters allege it is, illegitimate, so long as it were performing as required, most people would be inclined to leave well enough alone. It is only massive dissatisfaction with performance that permits large numbers of people to rally about the challenge to legitimacy. And the dissatisfaction with performance is, in effect, a rejection of the experts' claim to expertise. It is, therefore, a fundamental challenge to the working balance between professionalism and participation, for if the professionals do not have special competence, on what basis can they claim exemption from the normal political controls? Why should laymen defer to professionals when professionalism does not lead to effective performance? And, if there is no basis for deference, does not attention quite naturally shift from the dimension of expertise-effectiveness to the dimension of participation-legitimacy?

The preceding line of argument rather overstates the case many critics currently make. The tendency to defer to expertise remains, even though greatly weakened. But the argument does move in the direction here outlined, and hence at the very least, gives to the question of legitimacy a much more prominent place than it has hitherto been accorded.

The almost instinctive response of professionals to arguments such as these is simply, "Give us the tools, and we will do the job." The tools, once defined rather exclusively in terms of additional moneys or additional personnel, are now, however, increasingly defined as new structures—which is to say, the definition of the job itself is in dispute. In a dramatic concession to the demands of the constituents, many professionals have taken up the argument that present structures are ineffective, and need to be reformed not in order to bypass the professionals, but in order to liberate their expertise.

The fact is that it does not matter very much whether the attack on performance is valid or not. Validity, for purposes of systemic stability, is in the eye of the constituent. It might, perhaps, be possible to undertake a massive effort to persuade the critics that they are wrong, but the present disaffection is so profound, and the support given the disaffected by nonconstituent critics of the system is so intense, that, no evidence is very likely to persuade enough people to drop the argument. Further, *if* one indispensable ingredient in the success of an educational program is the confidence of the constituents in that program, it is not likely that, in the present climate, any program can be genuinely effective. Confidence has been withdrawn, and the first requirement for educational improvement is a restoration of confidence.

If this argument is correct, confidence cannot easily be restored through a renewal of effectiveness. At least for significant numbers of blacks, the issue has gone beyond that. Accordingly, if confidence is to be restored at all, if the required precondition to effectiveness is a restoration of legitimacy, then a new constitution must be written, attacking the problem of legitimacy directly. The most obvious change in the old order would be an increase in citizen participation. Thus: whether theorists are right or wrong in their views concerning participation is largely beside the present point; whether participation is desirable for its own sake or not, it is today necessary to restore needed legitimacy to the educational system. Without legitimacy, that system can hardly expect to become effective.

But: the preceding argument, it will be noted, is conditional. Only if it is true that educational effectiveness cannot be achieved in the absence of consumer confidence does the

rest of the statement necessarily follow. Since direct evidence
on the condition itself is not adequate to establish its validity,
those who continue to labor for increased effectiveness cannot
be dismissed as mistaken. They may be right; perhaps
improvement is possible even in the midst of a crisis of
legitimacy. So long as such a possibility exists, it is helpful
that our eggs are distributed in diverse baskets.

Participation and Control

So far, we have spoken only of participation, and have not
distinguished clearly between participation and control. High
levels of citizen participation in public school affairs have
traditionally been accepted, and even encouraged, by school
authorities. But control is quite a different matter, and the
more it is control which citizens seek, the more nervous
professionals tend to become. It is helpful here to point to two
other major social institutions which have analogous problems. In the American military system, the principle of
civilian control is well-established. Its acceptance by military
professionals is made somewhat easier by the readiness of
civilian authorities to accept the recommendations of the
professionals. Where those recommendations have been rejected—in the MacArthur-Truman dispute, for example—
major crises have ensued. But there is much greater theoretical
clarity about the proper limits on military autonomy than
there is with respect to the schools, partly because it is easier
to distinguish between substantive goals and implementary
techniques, and partly because the task of the military is
relatively discrete.

At the opposite extreme is the health delivery system of
the United States, and especially the case of the medical
profession. Doctors are, presumably, experts in curing people.
But, despite their expertise, the American health delivery
system is grossly ineffective. It fails to service adequately the
needs of large numbers of people in the society, and it does
only a mediocre job of preventive care. As a result, there has

been a growing demand for providing some sort of planning and administrative capability, external to the medical profession itself. The response of the professionals is vehemently hostile. Since, they claim, they know best how to do the job, it would be utter folly to place them under the direction of others less qualified than they.

The examples illustrate the need to distinguish between doing the job and defining the job that needs to be done. Doctors are more or less adept at curing people, but curing people is only one aspect of a health system. Military men are more or less adept at defeating enemies with force, but force is only one aspect of a foreign policy system. The question is not whether others are better qualified to do the job—clearly, they are not—but whether the professionals are by themselves competent to provide an adequate definition of the job. If they are not, then some system of control must be brought into being, a system which will both articulate the goals of the enterprise and act as a board of appeals to resolve conflicts between the professionals and their constituents.

Accordingly, it is insufficient to speak merely of participation. Inasmuch as education is a complicated and demanding enterprise, professional educators are required to implement the goals of the system. But inasmuch as education is a major societal investment, external systems of control are required to define the task and to assess the performance of the professionals.

This statement of principle, however, is not entirely adequate as an operational code. Great difficulties surround the task of assessment. Even at the most technical level—that is, even assuming that there were a general consensus on the appropriate criteria to be used—questions of measurement would still plague us. Moreover, there is no such consensus. The schools serve multiple functions and multiple constituencies; some of the functions are nearly impossible to measure, except intuitively, and many of the constituent groups place very different values on these functions. In the effort to clarify the confusion, many schools have retreated to peculiarly uninspired definitions of educational success, such as reading ability, dropout rates, and college entrance results. These are not irrelevant measures, but they barely begin to describe what the schools are about. It is for these reasons, in part, that efforts to introduce cost-benefit analysis into school management have had little impact; how, after all, do we accurately and consensually describe "benefits"?

In fact, conventional efforts to measure success may not only be confused, but may be deeply harmful. For if success comes to be defined as success in those aspects of schooling which are most easily measured, then it is a small step for the schools themselves to come to be about those same aspects, neglecting all the other functions which schools might be expected to fulfill.

Yet some controls are required, even if their basis is intuitive rather than scientific. In theory, such controls are provided by school boards. In practice, as we have seen, school boards find it difficult to operate effectively as control mechanisms, except in fiscal matters. More often than not, they operate instead as buffers between the professionals and their constituents, a far more passive role than genuine policy leadership implies. Nonetheless, if it can be agreed that schools should be controlled by nonprofessionals, in the general sense implied above, it becomes possible to move on to a more precise statement of the subordinate questions regarding control. Among the most important of these is defining the community that shall control.

Community and Neighborhood

Community control seems a plausible response to the present need of the educational system to restore its legitimacy in the eyes of its constituents—particularly its black constituents—and to endorse institutionally the enduring sense of community which many Americans appear to share. But neither derivative speaks clearly to the question of boundaries. At first blush, it might seem that each school, or group of schools, should, at least for some purposes, have its own mechanism of control, drawing upon the people who live near it, or the parents whose children are enrolled in it. But before accepting such a conclusion, we are required to distinguish between the neighborhood and the community. Community, at least as we have been using the term, suggests organic connection, a sense of shared destiny. As Nisbet points out,

> Community is founded on man conceived in his wholeness, rather than in one or another of the roles, taken separately, that he may hold in a social order. It draws its psychological strength from levels of motivation deeper than those of mere volition or interest. . . . [It] is a fusion of feeling and thought, of tradition and commitment, of membership and volition. It may be found in, or be given symbolic expression by, locality, religion, nation, race, occupation, or crusade. Fundamental to the strength of the bond of community is the real or imagined antithesis formed in the same social setting by the non-communal relations of competition or conflict, utility or contractual assent.[15]

Now it may be that this meaning of community should not be given official and institutional sanction in America. Ethnicity, to take one example, is a powerful social fact, but that does not necessarily mean that it should become a political fact as well. Clearly, to give political sanction to ethnicity would be very different from merely providing some measure of autonomy to people who live near each other. For physical proximity is only sometimes coterminous with the boundaries of the organic community.

Here again, we encounter some theoretical ambivalence, most recently and comprehensively dealt with in litigation on legislative apportionment. The effect of Supreme Court decisions since Baker v. Carr (1962) has been to disallow, in legislative bodies at the state and lower levels, representation of any organized interest. The only allowable basis for apportionment today is population—i.e., one man, one vote. This seems a manifestly fair principle, and has been widely endorsed by liberal organizations. In addition to the fact that it sounds fair, it raises some hope that the long-standing rural bias of many state legislatures may be repaired. Taken literally, however, as the doctrine of "one man, one vote" has been taken by a number of state courts, as well as by the Supreme Court itself in subsequent decisions, it has interesting ramifications. The Supreme Court did not insist that all legislative districts within a given political jurisdiction be of exactly equal population; clearly, such a standard would have been impracticable. Instead, the Court held that districts must be as nearly equal in population as possible. In practice, this has meant that there might be, say, a five percent deviation from the mean size in any given district.

A recent reapportionment proposal of the Missouri legislature was invalidated by the United States Supreme Court (Kirkpatrick v. Preialer, decided on April 7, 1969). That proposal would have created districts with a maximum variance of only 3.13 per cent from the mean size. While the variance was well within limits which had been found acceptable elsewhere, the Court held the proposal invalid on the grounds that standards other than numbers alone had been used in drawing the boundaries. Specifically, the proposed reapportionment sought to avoid fragmenting areas with distinct social and economic interests, on the theory that such fragmentation would dilute the effective representation of historic interests. The Court, in striking down the plan, held that "to accept population variances, large or small, in order to create districts with specific interest orientations is antithetical to the basic premise of the constitutional command to provide equal representation for equal numbers of people." The objection, in other words, was not that the deviation was "too" great, according to some arbitrary standard, but rather that it was greater than it would have been had numbers alone guided the process. And the reason that it was greater than it need have been was that the legislature sought to preserve the political identity of certain historic interests in Missouri. Only if there were a fortuitous match between raw numbers and historical communities could the boundaries have been drawn around communities.

The interests in question in Missouri were largely economic. But one can easily imagine noneconomic interests which might form the basis for an apportionment plan. Race and religion are only two examples among many. The theoretical objection to any such recognition derives directly from that view of the polity which holds the basic building block of the political system to be the individual, rather than, say, the caste, or the family, or the economic interest. In addition to the theoretical objection, there is also a powerful practical consideration: if the system gives official recognition to communities of interest, where does the process begin, and where does it end? People group together with others in diverse formations; our economic mates are not necessarily, or frequently, our coreligionists, or our brothers, or our ideological bedfellows. Yesterday, women had only limited political interests as women; today, women are coming increasingly to share a political agenda with each other. How can the system know when an interest deserves to be recognized, and how can it deal with the problem of multiple memberships?

There are, perhaps, answers to these questions, but the answers are frightfully complicated, and the theoretical argument in favor of strict numerical equality is sufficiently persuasive so as to diminish, if not eliminate, interest in the practicability of alternative proposals. The net result is that, with the exception of the special status accorded the several states, in both the Electoral College and the United States Senate, the political system is forbidden, in apportioning legislative districts, from taking explicit account of communities of interest.

This line of reasoning does not necessarily apply to all the component parts of the system, since, if it can be shown that there are substantive reasons for recognizing interest-based groupings, the courts might permit exceptions to the general rule. Constitutional doctrine on such matters is far from settled, and the creation of school districts of different size, based on things other than numbers and geographic propinquity, or both, does not automatically dilute the equality pursued in the apportionment decisions. No analogy is intended; instead, the important point is that were schools organized around communities of interest, community control would be a dramatic exception to the basic, and general, governmental formula which informs almost all government structures.

Insofar as the thrust for their organization is an effort to assert the validity of the organic community, and inasmuch as the organic community is not identical with the neighborhood, we are faced with a dilemma. Shall we except the schools from the conventional rules, permitting them to be tied to communities rather than neighborhoods, or, tying them to the neighborhood, shall we sacrifice a major justification for community control?

To tie the schools to the organic community rather than the neighborhood would raise the same practical problems that we alluded to in connection with legislative apportionment, albeit in less complicated fashion. For, unlike legislative apportionment, there is no intrinsic reason why the delineation of communities of interest would have to be undertaken by a higher political authority. Instead, it would be perfectly possible for communities to define themselves, something which school-communities now do in the case of private and parochial schools. If such a procedure were generally adopted, there is every reason to believe that some communities would be based on neighborhood, some would be based on ethnicity, some, perhaps, on educational or political ideology. Unhappily, there is also every reason to believe that a large number would be based on race. It is one thing for blacks freely to choose other blacks as their brothers; it is quite another to have such a choice forced on them by white bigotry. Ethnic communities can only be benign where they are not an inescapable assignment. For white ethnics, there are sufficient polyethnic communities to satisfy this need for options. But for blacks, the absence of multiracial communities changes the nature and severity of the problem markedly. If people were entirely free to choose their community of interest for purposes of school selection, large numbers of whites, in the current climate, would adopt a negative principle of selection, defining their community as one excluding blacks. Some Negroes might choose to associate with predominantly white schools, but the provision of complete freedom to define the boundaries of the community would, in effect, provide whites with veto power over the entry of black students, a veto it seems likely they would exercise. And this seems a fatal flaw in such a system.

What, then, if the neighborhood were used as the basis for the community school? Even if most neighborhoods are not significant organic communities—and a substantial number are—neighbors do share certain interests, as neighbors. These are primarily instrumental interests; they deal with such matters as the adequacy of municipal services, public morality, recreation, and, of course, the schools. In fact, the school is the central tie in many neighborhoods; to deprive the neighborhood of the school as a focus might well lead to a serious dimunition of the sense of relationship which makes of some neighborhoods more than a random group of people. At the same time, by providing the neighborhood with genuinely significant responsibilities, we help to increase the sense of community. Moreover, if we rank American neighborhoods according to the degree to which they are also organic communities, we find that the demand for community control of the schools arises primarily from the most community-oriented neighborhoods. Space becomes an increasingly significant social variable as one moves nearer the bottom of the economic ladder; for blacks, whose spatial mobility is limited both by income and by race, the neighborhood boundary is often nearly identical with the communal boundary. That, after all, is why the term "ghetto' is useful.

It suggests both a physical border and a community of inter-est.

On balance, then, it would appear that the neighborhood is a somewhat less problematic base for the community school than the organic community. Still, it is not without problems. Local areas in American cities, if they are communities at all, are, for the most part, communities of limited liability. Geo-graphic mobility in America is significantly encouraged by the knowledge that to move to a new neighborhood does not require formal or informal induction ceremonies of serious quality. Controlling for class, one neighborhood is pretty much like another; even the neighbors themselves become interchangeable. Our neighbors do not expect much of us, save rudimentary courtesy, nor we of them. While such a lack of serious sentiment significantly undermines the possibility of genuine fraternity, it simultaneously increases the possibil-ity for personal freedom.

Were the neighborhood provided with a serious shared responsibility, the liability would be increased. As an antidote to urban anonymity, as a spur to genuine participation, the prescription seems useful. But we ought not underestimate the degree to which communities of limited liability have come to be valued as a core feature of the American way of life. Those who have special needs for the geographic ex-pression of organic ties may, of course, seek out the like-minded, and together create as intimate a community as they wish, but others either have long since left behind the organic community, or see no need to define it spatially. Were the system to shift dramatically away from the community of limited liability and towards relatively isolated fraternities, many people would be totally confused; so long accustomed to the suppression of fraternity, they are by now charactero-logically incapable of it.

Finally, the facts of residential segregation make the neigh-borhood nearly as exclusive (racially) a base as the organic community would likely be. While the neighborhood may, for several reasons, be less problematic than the organic community, it is, therefore, far from ideal; if our concern is with maximizing choice, external inducements and guarantees are required in order to insure the development of multiracial neighborhoods.

These caveats need not deter us for long just yet. The community school will not suddenly transform a neighborhood of isolates into a community of meaning; the more likely prognosis is for a marginal increase in neighborhood sentiment, and marginal increases are hardly a threat to the established culture. Moreover, it is important to recall that the community of limited liability is, in most respects, a middle-class phenomenon. It is intimately related to geographic mobility, and such mobility is of concern primarily to the more affluent. Indeed, such people may participate in meaningful communities, but their communities, as distinguished from those of the less mobile, are tied together by a more diverse array of media—professional conventions, journals, telephones. It is not necessarily that community has ceased to matter to them, but rather that space has ceased to matter. Whether it is necessary, or even desirable, to "free" others from the constrictions of space, or whether the urge to do so is merely a liberal conceit, are moot questions. Those who would object to endorsing the neighborhood as a politically relevant unit, at least with respect to the schools, on the grounds that neighborhoods should be treated as more incidental categories of classification, should remember that the affluent, both by virtue of their social status and by virtue of their ability and propensity to live in smaller suburbs, already have the opportunity to intervene in school politics. Indeed, a foremost argument of the proponents of community control of the schools is precisely that they seek no more than many Americans already enjoy.

Scale

There is, in fact, a more perplexing element in choosing between the geographic neighborhood and the organic community as the basis for the school system, and it becomes apparent as we confront the question of scale, a question we cannot avoid if the neighborhood is also to become a significant political jurisdiction. For there is no single definition of the neighborhood; for some purposes, it is the block, for others, the elementary school, for others it is defined by shopping patterns. The desire to convert neighborhood into community, to encourage fraternity, suggests an intimate neighborhood, one where people can recognize each other, one, perhaps, whose residents might all fit into the school auditorium. And such a definition accords with the apparent desire to recreate smallness, to rediscover the virtues of the small town.

The difficulty here is that those virtues crumble under close inspection. If, in our earlier discussion of community, we emphasized the virtues of fraternity, it is now time to call attention to its dangers.

> There is something about life in a small community that makes it less hospitable to divergent opinions than is the case in our urban centers. In the anonymity of city life it is much easier for deviant behaviors to flourish than in the goldfish bowl of a small community. In the large community there are sometimes so many goldfish that nobody bothers to look at them. In the small town a lone exotic specimen can be viewed with careful, critical, and occasionally devastating concern.[16]

Thus, against the image of the sturdy cohesiveness and grass roots democracy of the small town we must juxtapose the image of the oppressive, censorial, anti-libertarian small town. Both sets of terms describe the same phenomenon; the choice depends largely on the perspective of the beholder rather than the character of the phenomenon. Nor is it possible to inquire productively as to which image is the more accurate. Both are accurate, for the small town involves a trade-off between certain values no less than does the metropolis. In general, the smaller the society, the less opportunity there is for deviance, whether political or cultural, the more the majority exercises subtle—or explicit—tyranny. In return for a major sacrifice in liberty, a sacrifice which many people are perfectly willing, and even anxious, to make, the small community offers social support, a sense of belonging, an alternative to the uncertainties of autonomy. Yet those who would reflect nostalgically on the good old days of solidarity should bear in mind the treatment of eccentricity in those days, in those places. Solidarity was available only at a price.

The American political system has developed out of a very different perception. Since Madison, the system has been alert to the threat of tyranny, and has sought to defend against that threat. Let us recall the Madisonian argument: if we are concerned by a tyranny of the minority, a remedy is available in the principle of majority rule. But we need also to defend against majority tyranny. How can this be done?

> Either the existence of the same passion or interest in a majority must be prevented, or the majority, having such coexistent passion or interest, must be rendered, by their number and local situation, unable to concert and carry into effect schemes of oppression. If the impulse and the opportunity be suffered to coincide, we well know that neither moral nor religious motives can be relied on as adequate control.
>
> From this view of the subject it may be concluded that a pure democracy, by which I mean a society consisting of a small number of citizens, who assemble and administer the government in person, can admit of no cure for the mischiefs of fraction. A common passion or interest will, in almost every case, be felt by a majority of the whole; a communication and concert result from the form of government itself; and there is nothing to check the inducements to sacrifice the weaker party or an obnoxious individual.[17]

Madison's argument is a classic of American political thought; it is likely the single most important document in the history of that thought, and one of the most widely taught, read, and accepted. Insofar as it is accepted, the suggestion that small communities be given political power is a violation of the general understanding. Insofar as it is valid, the vision of community schools is seriously tarnished. And, to make matters worse, we can no longer be quite so sanguine as was Madison about the problem of minority tyranny. Even if we discount the existence of apathy, which permits minorities to exercise disproportionate power, an increasing propensity to threaten physical violence suggests frightening possibilities Madison may well have not been required to consider.

But if we accept Madison's reasoning, and further compromise the community school by encouraging districts large enough to contain substantial diversity, have we not sacrificed almost completely the goal of rediscovering at least a limited fraternity? Organic community implies shared values; diversity implies value dissensus. If diversity is required to defend against tyranny, then community is lost. If community is required to defend against impotence, tyranny is possible. And so it is that much of the attack against the community school has rested on the argument that small communities cannot be trusted to enforce the freedoms most of us hold central to the society. If, for example, the values of the community find a specific monthly magazine obnoxious, what is to prevent the community from removing that journal from the shelves of the school library? If a certain teacher is identified, outside the school, with an activity which offends a group vocal in the community, what is to prevent it from demanding that he be fired?

These kinds of questions can be answered, but it is important, before answering them, to acknowledge the degree to which they are put forward by serious people of honorable intent. They are not, as some would have it, merely a smokescreen for racism. Many people have long been concerned about the censorial policies of small town vigilantes, and they are, it seems to me, fully entitled to express equal concern for the possibility that community schools will encourage big city vigilantes. It is not sufficient to dismiss their argument by citing the persistence of vigilantism elsewhere, and it is unfair to imply that they seek to apply to the community-controlled school standards which are not operative elsewhere. From their perspective, those standards *should* apply everywhere. Accordingly, the argument must be answered on its merits.

One kind of answer is, most simply, that it would be no great problem were the community to tyrannize. As Robert Dahl has shown, Madison's use of the concept "tyranny" is very fuzzy, since it does not tell us which actions of a majority are to be viewed as tyrannical and which as benign.[18] If the values of a community are genuinely violated by a deviant journal or a deviant teacher, why should the community not be entitled to censor the one or censure the other? If it does not have that right, how can we pretend that schools are intended, even in part, to transmit the values of the community? Which community? The large, amorphous, lowest-common-denominator-oriented national community? What happens to diversity under such conditions? Surely, some defense against egregious violations of the national ethic, such as it is, or of the national interest, such as it is, may be developed. Beyond that, ought not communities be permitted their own standards?

A second answer argues not from theory, but from practice. It holds that the schools, as presently organized, are in fact the "property" of a community—largely a middle-class community of college graduates who define the curriculum, the goals, the techniques of public education. In other words, the schools, as presently structured, do not insure that diversity which Madison sought; instead, they are of and by a specific group, a group with interests which may not match the interests of those whom they are ostensibly for. Community schools, the argument continues, would serve to open the system to a more diverse array of values, and not to close it. From the perspective of the system as a whole, options would be increased. And while, from the perspective of the individual school, there would be no increase in diversity, neither would there be a significant decrease. If majority tyranny is a real problem, then it is a problem which affects schools today. Worse, the majority that today tyrannizes is an alien majority; vis-à-vis the communities now seeking control over the schools their children attend, it is a minority.

The issues raised here speak not only to the question of scale, but also to the issue of district boundaries. Insofar as the system seeks to maintain some sort of balance between the competing values of liberty and fraternity, it must also seek a balance between social diversity and homogeneity. It is true, of course, that many urban neighborhoods are socially homogeneous, and, therefore, that to base the school on the neighborhood is to emphasize community. So, too, to require heterogeneous schools is to constrict community. Our problem is that we have powerful reasons to seek to maximize two values at once, and it is not at all clear that the two values are compatible.

Evidently, the concept of fraternity is more closely associated with the concept of society, while the concept of liberty is more closely associated with the concept of the polity. The one implies organic relationship, the other contractual relationship. The central theoretical dilemma of public education is precisely this: we have not made up our minds as to whether education is primarily a function of society or primarily a function of the state. If of the society, we would expect emphasis on affective relations, on community traditions, on particular truths. If of the state, we would expect emphasis on affective neutrality, on self-control, on universal truths. What we find, owing to our ambivalence, is a system full of internal contradictions, contradictions which tend to be solved by stressing organizational behaviors. Such behaviors inhibit both individual idiosyncracy, on the one hand, and meaningful human relationships, on the other. By avoiding the potential parochialism of fraternity and the potential eccentricity of liberty, they promote adaptive efficiency. And efficiency is both a common and a convenient replacement for genuine value commitment.

Clearly, education antedates the state, and is a primary means by which societies seek to insure their survival. In the small society, the division between the agencies of the state and the agencies of the community was rarely clear, nor, if clear, was the state necessarily pre-eminent. But we are dealing now with large and complex societies, containing within themselves diverse communities, whose relations with one another tend to be governed and adjudicated by the state. In its efforts at managing diversity, the state has an obvious and major interest in the content of education, since it could not tolerate a situation in which the schools not only mirrored, but reinforced, the societal fragmentation.

There are, in general, two ways for the state to protect its interests. The one involves direct intervention in the management of the schools, a system preferred by most European countries, but rejected in the United States. The other is to rely on the diffusion of a national ethic powerful enough to insinuate itself into the private ethic of all, or most, subcultural groupings. There is, of course, the danger that what begins as insinuation will end up by overwhelming and destroying diversity in its wake, but between the threat of fragmentation and the threat of uniformity, the state is bound to opt for uniformity. The wonder is that substantial diversity remains for those who energetically pursue it. More correctly, for *some* of those who pursue it. Energy is not enough; resources, too, are required, including political and economic power, and a reasonably sure sense of what is being sought. Though the odds are with the state, the community is not without recourse, given the American tradition. But the question must not be seen as how the final victory of one side or the other can be insured. Rather, the question is how balance can be maintained. And concern for balance points to specific diagnoses rather than general ones. Here the state seems overbearing, there the community seems stifling. Each instance, therefore, requires unique address.

These theoretical musings are, in part, given concrete shape in several sections of the Bundy Report. At various places in that report, the following points are made:

1. The number and shape of new districts should be determined with great care in order to insure boundaries that are both educationally sensible and socially sound. The determination should take account of such factors as: sense of community (and) diversity in composition of student population.[19]

2. The proposed reorganization would have built-in safeguards against movement towards still greater segregation of New York City schools. For example, if the central agency should reinstitute its open enrollment program, Community School Districts with empty seats in mainly white schools would be required to receive Negro and Puerto Rican pupils from other districts.[20]

3. The most important deterrent to segregation is quality education. Communities which achieve high levels of pupil performance—in schools that have a favorable climate for learning—will be the strongest possible magnet to draw *all* kinds of parents back to the city.[21]

4. [A major source of concern regarding the concept of community schools is the fear of provincialism. There are adequate defenses against this. Moreover,] within limits, fulfillment of highly localized interests may be a distinct advantage, giving residents a proprietary interest in the schools and enhancing the community climate and the motivation of children. Besides, it is not unreasonable that a district whose population is of predominantly Puerto Rican ancestry should spend additional school funds on Spanish-language instruction, or that a mainly Negro neighborhood should give extra emphasis to African culture or the history of the American Negro. . . . Many students of education hold, in fact, that it is pedagogically desirable for the curriculum to contain subject matter that is immediately relevant to the learner.[22]

There is obviously some tension between the stated goals of "sense of community" and "diversity in the composition of student population." That tension is illustrated in citations 2 through 4 above. Let us suppose, for example, that the fourth point, endorsing community-oriented curricula, is taken seriously. Under such circumstances, is it likely that parents who have fled the city, a group made up predominantly of whites, will return to enroll their children in these schools, no matter how excellent their "secular education"? Or, suppose that not only Puerto Ricans and blacks, but many other racial and ethnic groups develop curricula "immediately relevant to the learner"—to wit, we infer from the examples, ancestral languages, ethnic history, and so on. What happens, then, to the Negro and Puerto Rican pupils discussed in the second point, those who would be bussed into white districts? Shall they be encouraged to study Italian, or Chinese? And, if they are not so encouraged, and remain relatively few in number, will they not feel still more alien than they do today? For they will no longer be attending schools with curricula essentially interchangeable, as the curricula of state schools are. Rather, they will be attending schools with a definitive style, a style based on a communal solidarity they cannot share.

In confronting these questions, the New York State legislature has required heterogeneous districts; it has opted for diversity rather than community, an option wholly in keeping with the instinctive theoretical bias of the system, and the purposes of the state. For heterogeneous districts enable the system to avoid recognizing community as an educationally relevant phenomenon. But in the present climate, such a choice is likely to be interpreted by blacks as a violation of the entire thrust towards community control, which derives from very different purposes. In the end, it is not possible to discuss the virtues and liabilities of community control of the schools as an abstract theoretical question, as if it had nothing whatever to do with the racial crisis in America. When blacks urge community control, they do not do so because it is an appealing political philosophy, but because they see it as a solution to urgent problems their children face. And when they seek to solve those problems, the community they have in mind is the community of blacks. To appeal to other values, however compelling such values may be, is to subvert the special meaning which "community" is coming to have for black people, and the special purposes for which they seek community control. Smaller school districts, with a greater opportunity for parental involvement, might help make the schools better in general, but if they were to include heterogeneous populations, they would not be blacker. Since, it is argued, the only way to insure that the schools will be better specifically for blacks is to see to it that they are *both* blacker and controlled by the community, mere reduction in size is an inadequate response.

Perhaps the best that we can do to work our way out of the theoretical confusion is to adapt Berelson's view of the political system to the social system in general. *De facto,* society includes a great variety of communities, ranging from the highly organic to the highly incidental. Some people, perhaps, are trapped in a community they would not freely choose, yet cannot find the strength to leave. But there is no reason to suppose that most people do not get pretty much what they want. So long as the community is essentially a voluntary form of association, and so long as at least some communities are very loosely structured, and welcoming to newcomers, movement is possible. The liberal notion that organic communities are intrinsically bad reflects a very superficial understanding. If some people prefer neighborhoods of limited liability, seeking more organic ties elsewhere than the neighborhood or not at all, that is their business. And if others choose to live their lives within the bosom of the closed community, that is theirs.

The only issue that arises is whether the derivative freedom of groups to define themselves does not inevitably leave some people out in the cold. If it does, then the power of groups to draw their own boundaries must somehow be limited. The haunting spectre of walled neighborhoods might be more frightening if the only bases of community in America were race and ethnicity. But the increasing propensity of people to define their communities in terms of cultural styles and income levels makes possible a greater flexibility. If, in short, powerful theoretical arguments can be raised on both sides of an issue, ought not the benefit of the theoretical doubt be given those whose stake is greatest and whose needs are most urgent—a position which points to ceding black people themselves the right to define the nature and boundaries of the community.

With one exception: if it can be shown that education cannot happen properly unless it is based on diversity—if black children cannot learn unless they learn together with whites, or if working class children do not learn unless they learn with middle class children—the justification for placing the schools under the authority of those organic communities which seek such authority fails. This is an important matter, and goes to the heart of the community control debate as a problem in educational theory, to which we now turn.

CHAPTER FOUR

COMMUNITY CONTROL AND EQUAL EDUCATION

I N TURNING to a consideration of the educational consequences of community control of the schools, we arrive at an
area where there is both an abundant literature and a dearth
of data. Emotional investment in public education being what
it is, both opponents and proponents of community control
have felt it necessary to defend their positions on educational
grounds. This has been true even where their behavior suggests that other considerations, such as the protection of
established traditions and interests or access to political
power, appear pre-eminent. Yet, because community control
in the sense intended by the black community has yet to be
established on more than an experimental basis, the arguments cannot be based on adequate empirical data. Thus
neither side has a compelling body of evidence to sustain its
position.

Introduction

There are two broad lines of educational argument regarding community control, the one proceeding from what is
desirable for education in general, the other from a judgment
of the special needs of urban blacks. Our own interest is with

the second, since we are here primarily concerned with the debate over community control as an urgent matter of public policy, and not with the various proposals for general educational reform now current, of which community control is one. Nor are we interested in a discussion of the question of "optimal" school district size. It is, of course, true that a move towards community control of the schools would necessarily involve a significant reduction in the size of many urban school districts, but it is equally true that such reduction could be implemented without turning school management over to nonprofessionals. Indeed, a number of the more radical reform proposals now being discussed promise major reductions in district size, in some cases making each individual school its own district, without in any way endorsing greater parental or citizen participation, let alone control. As we have already noted, the goal of administrative decentralization and the goal of community control ought not be confused.

The real question that is raised by advocates of community control is less related to size (how large the district shall be) than to character (around what "kinds" of people the district boundaries shall be drawn). Once again, when we use the term community, we mean something that approximates an organic group, and not merely an *ad hoc* political jurisdiction created to meet an instrumental-administrative need. Even if we accept the neighborhood as the most feasible basis for defining the boundaries of the community school, we do so knowing that the neighborhoods of special interest to us are not so far from the organic community. Indeed, that may be why the residents of such neighborhoods take the issue so seriously.

Some advocates of community control abet the confusion by arguing that they seek no more than suburban parents already enjoy. Since, it is alleged, suburban schools are both markedly better than urban schools, and, typically, smaller and more accessible, smallness and accessibility must have beneficent effects. Unfortunately for both suburban children and this argument, however, many suburban schools provide only mediocre education, and those that excel may do so for a variety of reasons unrelated to size—higher per capita investment in education, better educated parents, and so on. Nor even were accessibility of the schools deemed a virtue for its own sake, is it clear that such accessibility is due either to small size or to an ideology of openness rather than to higher status of some suburban parents and their greater experience with, if not desire for, control over their environment. Finally, a continuing difficulty with the suburban analogy is the excellence, amidst all the educational crises, of any number of big-city schools.* In almost every major urban center, there are several schools (at least) which match, and even exceed, the very best suburban schools. And these schools are part of "impossible" systems. The dreariness of many suburban systems teaches us that system smallness is not a sufficient guarantee of excellence; the excellence of many urban schools teaches us that system smallness is not a necessary condition either.

Inasmuch as the demand for community control has become an urgent political question because it has been put forward as a response to black demands for quality education, it is in that context that we consider it. And in that context, quite clearly, the central proposition is that black children are not adequately served under current arrangements. Some suggest community control as a way of changing our understanding of educational success; it is not, they argue, that black children are doing poorly in any absolute sense, but only relative to the very narrow definition of success employed by most systems. What looks like failure according to that definition might well look like success by some other definition. Others contend that educational procedures must be changed in order to meet the special needs of black children, but that present structures, whether because of organi-

---

* By "excellence," we mean according to conventional standards—of which more later.

zational sclerosis or racist beliefs, are incapable of such change. Whatever the exact, or inexact, arguments, the dismal statistics of educational gap between blacks and whites are compelling, and their political salience growing. Accordingly, no one argues with the general proposition that we are required, in order to achieve both moral and political salvation, to close that gap. But in order for us to understand whether community control is a plausible device for closing the gap and moving towards equality of educational opportunity, we must first explore the meaning, in this context, of equality.

Educational Equality and the Black-White Gap

Not very long ago, it would not have been necessary to devote much attention to this question. Equality of educational opportunity was generally understood to imply that a free education was to be made available to all children, and that there could be no invidious distinctions in the facilities used to provide such education.[1] Even so simple a definition gave rise to serious problems, for the American tradition of local budgeting for schools led to massive differences in per pupil expenditures, even within states, and even within single school districts. Such differences were not, however, challenged in the courts until recently, and even then, curiously, not as an outgrowth of the School Desegregation Cases,[2] but rather as a consequence of the Supreme Court's decisions on reapportionment.[3] In the Brown decision, the Court had held that the opportunity for education had to be "made available to all on equal terms." The issue at hand, however, was not general inequality, but the specific inequality visited on blacks through segregation. The Court made it clear (in its decision in Griffin v. County School Board) that different school districts within a state might continue to support their educational facilities at different levels (that is, might provide unequal educational facilities), holding only that such differences could not be based on racial criteria.[4]

But in the reapportionment cases, the Supreme Court

held that citizens of a state could not be discriminated against because of arbitrary political boundaries. The constitutionally protected equality in voting rights could not be diluted by the accidental misfortune of living in a relatively populous, and hence underrepresented, district. Since education, in the Brown decision, had been declared a constitutionally protected right, the apportionment cases gave rise to the question of whether those arbitrary boundaries called school districts were any more to be sanctioned, where inequity between districts existed, than the legislative districts that the Court had found unconstitutional. The question was given added power after the Court handed down its decision in Griffin v. Illinois, a case dealing with the rights of indigent defendants.[5] In that decision, the Court held that governments are forbidden to discriminate against the poor—specifically, that an indigent defendant cannot be denied his right to appeal merely because he cannot afford the cost of a transcript of the trial proceedings. In summary, then, the Court has held that discrimination cannot be based on race, on intrastate political boundaries, or on wealth. This set of discrete decisions has given rise to an effort to bring them all together and apply them to education, thereby eliminating the inequities in per pupil expenditure which exist in almost every large school district and in every state.

It can be shown that, in general, per capita expenditure for predominantly black schools is less than per capita expenditure in predominantly white schools, even within the same districts.[6] (Although it should be noted that Federal aid has had an impact on such inequity, in some cases resulting in higher expenditures in predominantly black schools.) But it can also be shown that even were such inequities eliminated, much of the educational gap between black and white would remain. One analysis, for example, finds that were the level of teaching resources devoted to Negroes to be raised to the level currently devoted to whites, the gap between Negro and white verbal achievement in the twelfth grade would be reduced by a little more than 25 percent.[7] Such a reduction cannot be dismissed as trivial, but it does suggest that even the elimination of inequities in educational input in the schools would not, of itself, eliminate the inequity in educational performance. Accordingly, much attention has of late come to be devoted to the question of how educational equality shall be defined.

The most serious blow to the doctrine that equality should be defined in terms of inputs, or resources, derives from the work of James S. Coleman and his colleagues in their report, "Equal Educational Opportunity."[8] The Coleman data show that "variations in the facilities and curricula of the schools account for relatively little variation in pupil achievement insofar as this is measured by standard tests." Despite the fact that many questions have been, and can be, raised regarding the adequacy of the data base from which this conclusion derives, it has now come to be widely accepted as valid. The conclusion, therefore, appears warranted that if society has a legitimate concern in reducing, or eliminating, the gap in educational attainment, it cannot rest with a policy of eliminating inequity in investment.

Actually, there is significant precedent for moving beyond a kind of mechanical fixation on strict equality in resources. A half century ago, Frank Thompson, then superintendent of the Boston public schools, maintained that,

> We cannot ignore the arguments for some sort of special educational provision for immigrant children. The motive is similar to that which has prompted us to make special provision for various kinds of atypical children. We wish in the schools to furnish an equality of educational opportunity; but we can no longer deny the fact of individual variation of powers and abilities, and the schools cannot bestow an equality of benefit through the same ministrations to all children; children equipped with lesser gifts by nature must be given more by nurture.[9]

It is not a very long leap from the belief that the schools have a special responsibility to cope with inequalities of "nature" to the doctrine that they bear a responsibility to compensate for inequalities caused by poverty, or other disabling circumstances. In the last several years, the argument has been elaborately developed by Coleman, in a series of articles published after the appearance of the EEO report.[10]

Coleman's argument, in effect, is that genuine equality of opportunity requires that the schools produce equal results. Our focus must shift from the resources which go into education to the product that comes out. Or, centrally, "the schools are successful only insofar as they reduce the dependence of a child's opportunities on his social origins."[11] This position can be defended on several grounds. First, it may be claimed that unless the schools produce equal results, we are entitled to presume that they do not, in fact, provide equal resources. After all, learning capacities are not so very different as to cause the massive inequality in results we see today, and the history of public school discrimination is so patent that suspicion of claims that it has been eliminated is a perfectly plausible stance. Coleman, however, does not base his argument on that line of reasoning. Evidence regarding preschool differences between blacks and whites suggests, instead, that the social and family backgrounds of poor blacks disable them even before they reach school. It is this difference in "starting points" which the schools, if their promise of equality is to be taken seriously, must overcome: "Equality of educational opportunity implies, not merely "equal" schools, but equally effective schools, whose influences will overcome the differences in starting points of children from different social groups."[12]

At first glance, this seems a noble pursuit, surely far more humane than the mere provision of comparable facilities to all children. But we encounter immediately the difficulty of defining how equality of effectiveness shall be measured. However limited a goal, equality of resources has one major virtue: it provides a fairly precise measure. But what does it mean, operationally, to insist that the schools insure that educational attainment be independent of family and social background? No one has proposed that each individual child should perform at precisely, or even approximately, the same level. Instead, the proposal must be taken to mean that disabilities now associated with membership in certain disabled social groups be removed. The appropriate measure of success, then, is whether members of such groups distribute themselves, with respect to educational performance, in roughly the same way as members of nondisabled groups. Specifically, it should become impossible to infer, from a child's performance in school, his group membership—and vice versa. Since we assume that natural abilities are randomly distributed among people, independent of their group membership, to free children from that membership would be to insure that achievement in school would reflect only innate capacity.[13]

Coleman is silent on the question of freeing children of traditionally overachieving groups from dependence on their social origins, but we are most likely safe in assuming that he would not endorse such a goal. What he has in mind, presumably, is not making education independent of social origins in general, but, rather, making education independent of disabling social origins. We can be still more specific: some origins are idiosyncratically distributed, and not characteristics of groups per se. A neurotic household, for example, may inhibit learning ability. But that is not what the Coleman proposal is intended to deal with. Coleman proposes an attack, by the schools, on those disabling social origins which are related to group membership.*

There is substantial evidence to support the position that some groups are, indeed, seriously disabled by an impover-

---

* If we were to take literally the unmodified statement that educational attainment should be independent of social origin, an effective strategy might be to retard the educational development of those who now perform relatively well. This could be accomplished by providing them with inferior educational opportunities, something the system might find easier than improving the quality made available to the disabled. Obviously, then, equality is not the only goal of the system. May it be that it in fact conflicts with other goals?

ished educational environment. Both experimental and aggregate evidence confirm this fact. And the major groups so affected are blacks and poor people. It does not, however, follow automatically that the schools can, or should, seek to overcome these crippling circumstances. One might argue, for example, that if it is life circumstances which determine life styles, and life styles in turn which determine learning capacity, the simplest approach to equality would be to attack differences in life circumstance. Surely an attack on the disease is more plausible than an attack on the symptom. To which the response is that nothing in the doctrine of equal effectiveness speaks against an effort to close the gap in circumstance. But until that gap is closed, the schools cannot afford merely to shrug their shoulders. Schools currently compound the societal inequity, when they should help ameliorate it. Moreover, there are times when to relieve the symptom is to cure the disease; if the schools were to be held to a standard of equal effectiveness, societal inequities would be reduced, since the poor and the black would have a much better chance of breaking the cycle of poverty.*

The more serious difficulty with the doctrine of equal effectiveness is that there may be significant differences among social groups that are not particularly disabling. Not all differences among groups are malignant, and we are required to ask whether some of those differences now classified as disabling may be so classified only because our educational standards are overly narrow. This question, in fact, is one of the prominent arguments put forward by some advocates of community control, who believe that a system dominated by middle-class values defines educational success so narrowly that it cannot appreciate the genuine achievements of non-middle class children.

---

* But Stephan Michelson holds that even if Negroes and whites were provided equal education, both quantitatively and qualitatively, the income disparity between the two groups would be cut by no more than one-half. See his "Equating Racial Incomes: On the Efficacy of Employment and Education Policies" (The Brookings Institution, 1967 [Mimeographed]).

Further, if we agree that some differences among groups are acceptable, how can we distinguish between those which are and those which are not? This problem is best illustrated by an unhypothetical analogy, derived from higher education, an analogy introduced in an earlier chapter. As noted there, many now argue that only a black college student population equivalent in size to the number of college-age blacks in the general population would constitute sufficient proof of equality of opportunity at the college level. Thus, if one out of eight Americans between the ages of eighteen and twenty-one is black, then one out of eight college students should be black. Such a position assumes that the desire to attend college is equally distributed among all groups. But suppose that desire is not equally distributed? Must we conclude that any group that does not choose to attend college at a rate equal to its numbers in the society is disabled? We know, for example, that the patterns of college attendance vary quite markedly from group to group; Italians attend at about half the rate that Irish do, and Jews at about three times the rate of Irish. It is possible, of course, that some of the difference is accounted for by financial ability. But even if college attendance were cost-free, it is likely that significant differences would remain.

Moreover, college attendance rates for the white population are, obviously, a statistical artifact. If, say, one-third of all the available age cohort is in fact enrolled in college, that one-third may include two-thirds of the members of one group, and only one-sixth the members of some other group. Thus, to argue that equality in attendance rates between blacks and whites is a significant measure of equality is to imply that the standard for equality should be derived from a mean composed of very diverse elements, and should be independent of the actual aspirations of blacks. It might be the case that blacks, if uninhibited by financial and educational deprivation, would choose to attend college far more often, say, than Italians do, but because Italian attendance rates are calculated as part of the white mean, the standard for black-white equality would be depressed. Or it might be that blacks would not, in conditions of genuinely free choice, choose to attend college very often; in that case, to insist on the white standard as a measure of equality would be to impose alien values on the Negro.

The issue is, assuredly, simpler with respect to the public schools, since college attendance is, at least formally, defined as an option in the society, whereas public school attendance is compulsory. The society defines public schooling as a universal good, and even people who might object to it are required to accept society's definition. But what of specific patterns of performance within the public schools? Given the minority status of Negroes, national norms will always depend critically on the performance of whites. It can be argued that such norms are applicable to blacks only if one of two conditions prevails: either there are no significant differences in performance between white groups, indicating that performance is independent of subculture,* or there are differences between white groups, and these differences are viewed as socially undesirable. Under the second condition, we might, for example, find that one white group (not merely a random assortment of white children) has a level of reading significantly above the national norm, a second group at that norm, and a third group significantly below the norm. Not all such deviations from norms are regarded by the society as intrinsically dangerous, but, where performance in a given area is so regarded, we can conclude that the "white" norm is, essentially, independent of whiteness; society has defined some minimum standard, and all children should be helped to meet that standard.

There is only one area where such a standard reigns, and that is reading ability. One may question whether the acceptance of reading as the central measure of educational attainment is a function of the need to know how to read or of the relative ease with which the ability is measured, but that does not appear a particularly fruitful line of inquiry. Reading

---

* This condition does not prevail. See page 106.

skills are commonly regarded as critical, and even if one were to adopt as a more proximate standard for public school performance the doctrine that blacks should be helped to perform at the reading level of that white group which has the lowest achievement, but is not discriminated against, there would still be a long way to go before the gap would close.

But even if reading ability does provide a rough standard of equal performance, we must emphasize that it is almost the only such standard. In other areas, continuing differences between blacks and whites may reflect subcultural patterns which are 1) *not* related to the environmental deprivation of blacks, or 2) which, if related, are in any event benign, or 3) which, if not benign, are malignant only by an overly constricted definition of educational success. Where subcultural patterns are not caused by environmental (or other) deprivation, it is doubtful that the schools are required to work towards their eradication; certainly nothing in constitutional doctrines of equality so suggests. Where the differences between groups, whatever their origin, are benign, such as would be the case, say, where one group excelled at verbal skills and another at mathematical skills, once again, neither the society nor its educational agents are permitted to reward the one and penalize the other. And where the differences are defined as malignant, as would be the case, for example, were mathematics regarded as socially useful and verbal ability as superfluous, we are bound to ask whether the definition itself is not wanting, is not merely a reflection of the distinctive cultural pattern of those who define what is useful and what superfluous.

We may summarize the preceding discussion as follows: were educational ability randomly distributed throughout the society, the goal of equal educational opportunity would be adequately served by insuring that all students were provided comparable educational facilities, including compensatory programs for individuals in educational difficulty. Unfortunately, learning ability is not randomly distributed; it does correlate with group membership. Our chief societal concern is with those groups which are educationally disabled, whether by virtue of poverty or racial discrimination. If members of such groups are to be offered genuine equality, we cannot rest with the simple provision of equal resources, though even that modest goal has yet to be achieved. (In fact, as the data in the Coleman Report show, such equality would have rather little effect on learning.) We are required, instead, to adopt a standard of equal effectiveness, a standard which would insist that the schools do whatever is necessary to free disabled children of their disabling origins. Such a standard is enormously difficult to define with precision; it is even difficult to define conceptually. Nonetheless, it is the only meaningful way of approaching genuine equality. At the very least, we conclude, we now have a definition of the lower boundary of equality—equal resources—and a definition of its upper boundary—equal outcomes. And neither condition is met today.

Integration, Compensation, and Equality

In what way is a discussion of equal education opportunity related to the debate over community control? After all, every serious commentator on the schools, whether he supports or opposes community control, endorses equality of opportunity, even if more minimally defined than above. Advocates of community control argue only that present structures are incapable of providing such equality, while their critics, whether supporters of present arrangements or of still other reform proposals, hold that there are more proximate ways of approaching equality than community control.

We have already noted one way in which the issue of equality is linked to the issue of community control. If present evaluations of educational performance are culture-bound, reflecting not general social purposes but the dominance of a particular group in defining performance, then community control is a plausible way of diversifying the definition. In this view, giving control over the schools to subcultural groupings would insure that the standards of success would reflect, in each case, the values of the controlling subculture. Thus, for example, one leading proponent of integration argues that "children of all backgrounds tend to do better in schools with a predominant middle class milieu."[14] It is possible, however, that such a finding does not originate in a special aptitude of middle-class children, but rather in the fact that standards of educational success tend to be defined by middle-class teachers and administrators.

In fact, the dominance of middle-class values is sometimes used as an argument for integration, as witness Thomas Pettigrew:

> Broadly speaking, public education serves society by preparing the individual (1) to maintain himself adequately through participation in a useful occupation, (2) to augment his productive potential, and (3) to cope with and understand himself. Segregation of the Negro, whether *de jure* or *de facto,* acts to the detriment of all three of these aims. And the criteria for evaluating adequacy are those favored by the dominant segment of American society—the white middle class. Apart from class complications, then, unbalanced schools defeat the broader goal of public education by failing to communicate to the Negro child the true standards by which he will surely be judged later.[15]

Serious questions can be raised regarding the relationship between preparing the individual "to cope with and understand himself" and racial integration, but that is not our concern at the moment. What Pettigrew shows us, in the present context, is that the premise of middle class dominance need not lead to the conclusion of community control. It is in this sense that community control emerges as a radical doctrine, for it, too, diagnoses an imbalance in power relationships, but, instead of urging that that imbalance be accepted as a basis for educational policy, it proposes instead to redress the imbalance. Excepting once again those disabilities which almost everyone agrees are educationally harmful, the remedy proposed by advocates of community control is to permit broader participation, and hence more eclecticism, in defining educational success.

But still more comprehensive linkages between the discussion of equality and the debate over control can also be identified. Let us review the Coleman argument: first, educational facilities show very little relationship to educational performance. The primary sources of educational inequality appear, instead, to lie in the home and the social environment. This is verified by data which show that inequalities exist even before children reach school age. Next, the schools abet the original inequality. How do they do this? Because schools tend to be culturally homogeneous, the originally disabling culture is simply reinforced in the schools which disabled students attend. But if this is so, then the achievement of equality depends on the schools being oriented about some culture other than the culture of origin. Specifically, Coleman finds that disabled students do best when they are in classrooms with middle-class children. With respect to the issue of race, this means that racial integration is required in order to achieve equality; there are not enough middle-class black children to "go around," so poor black children will have to be integrated with middle class white children. Otherwise, the poor will attend school with each other, and their disabling origins will simply be reinforced by the school experience. In Coleman's words,

> A pupil's achievement is strongly related to the educational backgrounds and aspirations of the other students in the school. . . . Children from a given family background, when put in schools of different social composition, will achieve at quite different levels. . . . The principal way in which the school environments of Negroes and whites differ is in the composition of their student bodies, and it turns out that the composition of the student bodies has a strong relationship

to the achievement of Negro and other minority pupils.*[16]

In short, genuine equality cannot be achieved without schoolroom integration across class lines; given black and white class distribution, such integration requires also racial integration. Without such integration, equality will not happen.

The Coleman position in this regard is based chiefly on data regarding educational performance, as measured in quite traditional ways. There exists, as well, a somewhat different line of reasoning which points to the same conclusion. Even if it were theoretically possible to imagine strict educational equality resulting in (*de facto*) segregated schools, the argument goes, the black children who attend such schools inevitably suffer psychological damage. Such damage, while not within the traditional definition of educational performance, is clearly a matter for social concern, and cannot be tolerated. This line of reasoning has been especially popular with the courts, although a number of decisions fail to distinguish between educational and psychological consequences of discrimination. One ruling (by Judge Julius Hoffman) holds that:

> School segregation, whatever the cause, has the effect of stigmatizing Negro pupils and retarding their educational development. The mere fact of separation encourages invidious comparison; and the false conclusion

---

* Henry Dyer registers an important reservation to this section of the Coleman report. "There is nothing in the Coleman data," he says, "that can justify such an inference. The Coleman study contains no data at all on the effects that might accrue from 'putting' minority pupils with different kinds of schoolmates. It is one thing to suppose that a pupil's attitudes and behavior reflect those of the peer group in which, because of innumerable circumstances, including possibly his own predilections, he happens to be; it is quite another thing to infer that if he is moved from one group to another, his attitudes and behavior will change in predictable ways." See Dyer, "School Factors and Equal Educational Opportunity," *Harvard Education Review,* 38, No. 1 (Winter, 1968), pp. 38–56, esp. p. 53.

that the Negro pupil is inferior to the white pupil is tragically forced onto the black child himself through constant elaboration and repetition. He sees white parents removing their children from his vicinity as if to protect them from contagion, and he sees school boards and administrators creating separate isolation wards to contain him.[17]

And, in one of the most comprehensive court decisions on educational inequality, Judge Skelly Wright found as fact that "racially and socially homogeneous schools damage the mind and the spirit of all children who attend them—the Negro, the white, the poor and the affluent . . . whether the segregation occurs by law or by fact."[18]

Thus we have two lines of argument which converge in their agreement that equality requires racial integration. Coleman, eschewing the standard of equal resources, contends that the doctrine of equal effectiveness depends upon racial integration for its fulfillment, and the courts, unclear as to the standard by which equality should be measured, nonetheless contend that segregated schools are *ipso facto* unequal.

But if American communities tend to be both racially and class homogeneous, then the goal of integration is incompatible with the goal of community control. If schools "belong" to their communities, they will be only as integrated, whether by race or by class, as those communities—hence, not very integrated at all. The question that arises, then, is whether community control of the schools does necessarily point away from the goal of equal educational opportunity, as Coleman by implication, argues. For if it does, that would be a very serious drawback, to say the least, even if no constitutional problems were thereby raised.

Thus, if we are to make a serious effort to understand the educational consequences of community control, we are required to reassess the evidence that integration is an absolute requirement of equality, which means also to assess the evidence that has emerged from various efforts at "compensatory" education—that is, efforts to improve educational performance of the blacks and the poor *without* integration.

Such assessment is beyond our present scope. Few public policy questions have been so massively debated; the literature abounds with studies which point now this way, now that. The Coleman report, simply because it was so massive, so very much more comprehensive than any other, appeared for a while to settle the matter, but other studies have since disputed the Coleman findings, either by finding flaws in the report itself, or by presenting new data which, it is claimed, show different results. The central reservation to the Coleman position is that adequate models of compensatory education, let alone community control, have yet to be realized on a scale sufficient to warrant the conclusion that compensation cannot work.

In some degree, the continuing effort to buttress the case for compensation, as opposed to integration, is based on hopelessness. Since integration on a meaningful scale seems very far away, and, in some cities, demographically impossible, to insist that only through integration can equality be achieved is to hold that equality cannot be achieved. It is difficult to know how much of the support for compensatory programs, and even for community control, derives from this position, but it is safe to say that were integration a more realistic possibility, many people who now support non-integrated reform efforts would shift their position.

We do not here enter the argument between the integrationists and the nonintegrationists, on the grounds that the data are as yet inadequate to provide a decisive answer to the central question of equality of educational opportunity. Some will disagree vehemently with this judgment, believing that the Coleman report and a number of supporting studies have settled the matter. Yet it seems to me that there are several compelling reasons for reserving judgment here. First, the Coleman data are, withall, too fragmentary to serve as the basis for so important a decision. Second, and of special importance, compensatory programs on a scale as yet untried may provide evidence that integration is not an absolute necessity. All that has been thus far measured is what exists; since many proposed reforms have yet to be implemented, the evidence is necessarily incomplete. In addition, inasmuch as integration does seem fearsomely difficult to achieve, and we are, in any case, going to have segregated schools for some years to come, we must hold out the hope for the children, the parents, and the teachers involved in such schools that something approximating equality can be achieved in them. Finally, many blacks now insist that they deserve a chance to try their hand at improving the educational performance of black children. Given the history of discrimination visited on the black community, it seems reasonable to give them that chance; given the intensity of the demands, it seems politic as well—unless there are overwhelming educational arguments against so doing.

Let us assume that integration is not an absolute necessary condition for equality; then we can ask whether community control, which is only one of many possible reform proposals, seems a useful alternative, on educational grounds. Since the kind of community control we are talking about—control by cohesive, rather than purely instrumental, communities—has not been extensively tried, the argument must rest on theory rather than empirical data. Proponents of community control have offered a number of theoretical reasons for their position, including the alleged advantages that would result for black students by having black role models in positions of authority in the school, the ability of communities to make the curriculum more "relevant" to the lives, and interests, of their students, the need to replace teachers and administrators now tainted, however subtly, with racism, and to provide teachers who have a profound commitment to success. And these are only a small sample of the arguments that have been put forward. In most respects, as we have noted, it is not possible to confirm or disconfirm the arguments. Two, however, deserve special attention, the one because it has gained rather widespread currency, the other because it is unusually provocative, and suggests that integration might create difficult educational problems.

In 1965, Robert Rosenthal and Lenore Jacobson conducted an intriguing experiment in a public elementary school, later reported in their book, *Pygmalion in the Classroom*.[19] They told teachers in the school that certain children in their classes had been identified as "growth spurters" by means of the "Harvard Test of Inflected Acquisition." The test was a hoax, and the children identified as "spurters" had, in fact, been chosen at random. The purpose of the experiment was to test the relationship between teacher expectation and pupil performance. The results indicated that there was, indeed, a strong relationship between the two; in general, those students whom the teacher had been led to expect growth from, grew, and grew more, as measured by IQ tests, than others of whom the teacher did not have special expectations.

This result, when published, was widely acclaimed as evidence for the view that a major ingredient of academic success is teacher expectation. Since many teachers of poor blacks do not appreciate their students, and, allegedly, have very little hope that they can perform well, teachers sympathetic to the community must be recruited. And the only agency that can be relied upon to make the necessary judgment regarding such a criterion is the community itself.* The felicitous title of the Rosenthal-Jacobson work called to mind Liza Doolittle's poignant speech:

> You see, really and truly, apart from the things anyone can pick up (the dressing and the proper way of speaking, and so on), the difference between a lady and a flower girl is not how she behaves, but how she's treated. I shall always be a flower girl to Professor Higgins, because he always treats me as a flower girl, and always

---

* It evidently did not occur to anyone that if the expectations of others affected pupil performance, these expectations might well affect teacher performance as well. In a climate of suspicion and hostility towards teachers, the Pygmalion doctrine might profitably be extended to suggest that teachers will themselves come to expect failure —their own failure.

will; but I know I can be a lady to you because you always treat me as a lady, and always will.

The special appeal of this position is that it makes educational equality seem much easier to attain. No longer are we required to worry centrally about the continuing impact of environmental disadvantage; simply create a system which can provide teachers who will say to their students, in effect, that they are getting better in every way every day, and, eureka, the gap will vanish—or, at least, be narrowed.

As luck would have it, however, efforts to replicate the Rosenthal-Jacobson study have met with very limited success. The authors themselves report that in at least three subsequent efforts, the results were quite different from those obtained in the original experiment.[20] Nonetheless, the proposition that high expectation leads to improved performance is sufficiently compelling, and the data sufficiently supportive, to encourage further efforts along these lines. The more central question concerns how one can hope to change teacher expectations on more than an experimental basis. There is, after all, a limit to the utility of a nonexistent test. And teachers who may be willing to believe that some of their pupils are capable of growth are not necessarily willing to believe that of all their pupils. Nor is it clear that community control would have a greater impact on teacher expectation than other kinds of reforms. The chief advantage of community control, in this connection, is that it would provide the community with a kind of veto power over particularly pessimistic teachers. But such power might be, in various ways, grafted onto present structures as well. On balance, the Pygmalion findings speak more directly to other aspects of the educational process, and particularly to the potential hazards of ability tracking, than to the overall structure of the system.

More relevant to the community control debate are the unusually provocative findings of Gerald Lesser and his associates.[21] Lesser investigated patterns of mental abilities among six- and seven-year-old children from different social class and ethnic backgrounds. Four mental abilities (verbal ability, reasoning ability, number facility, and space conceptualization) were tested for middle and lower class children from four ethnic groups—Chinese, Puerto Rican, Negro, and Jewish. The original study was conducted in New York, and was later repeated in Boston, with two of the original four ethnic groups and an additional group of Irish children.

The design is intriguing, for it permits us to compare the impact of social class with the impact of ethnicity. Some years ago, Kenneth Clark wrote that "There is no evidence that there is any cultural factor that is relevant to the complexity of the learning process."[22] If Clark was correct, then we would expect social class to be a far more powerful predictor of mental ability than ethnicity, the cultural factor Clark had in mind. And Lesser does find that in each ethnic group, middle-class children consistently outperform lower-class children. Hence social class integration would seem to be a reasonable strategy for educational improvement.

But the more interesting, and less expected, finding of the Lesser study was that each ethnic group has a distinctive pattern of ability, and that pattern *does not change* with social class variation. The results are striking indeed, as can be seen in Figures 1 through 4. There is somewhat less difference among middle class children of different ethnic groups than among lower class children of those groups. That is, the scores of middle class children from the several groups resemble each other more than the scores of lower class children do. But this finding is overshadowed by the finding that ethnic patterns are highly durable across class lines.

This study provides the most impressive empirical evidence to date that subcultural patterns are not merely reflections of lower-class status, but a significant aspect of group life. Social class may be a leading determinant of the *level* of achievement, but the *pattern* of achievement is more a function of ethnic group. As Stodolsky and Lesser point out, such evidence suggests an educational strategy rather different from that proposed by Coleman.[23] If we follow Coleman, the measure of equal educational opportunity is equality of performance. Such performance assures us that achievement is independent of background. But Stodolsky and Lesser observe that:

> Since the data on patterns of intellectual functioning indicates that once the mental-ability pattern specific to the ethnic group emerges, social-class variations within the ethnic group do not alter the basic organization associated with ethnicity, this finding suggests that lower-class children whose social-class position is elevated would still retain the distinctive mental-ability pattern associated with their ethnic group. The implication is that no matter what manipulations are undertaken to modify the social-class positions of children within an ethnic group, the distinctive ethnic-group pattern of abilities will remain.[24]

The authors then go on to suggest that, once acquisition of basic minimum skills is guaranteed to members of all ethnic groups, a wise strategy might be to promote the special abilities of each group. The net result would be a highly uneven, and hence, unequal, distribution of talents. Thus to insist on equal performance might, in effect, be to insist that some groups operate from weakness rather than from strength, a policy which would be difficult both to defend and to implement.

If one accepts the Stodolsky-Lesser position that different ethnic learning patterns are both enduring and benign, it would appear to add a powerful argument in favor of community control. It is hard to imagine an ethnically integrated school sufficiently flexible to encourage each group in its own unique pattern; schools, having come to behave as organizations, are strongly biased towards uniformity and impersonal standards.

More specifically, juxtaposition of Stodolsky-Lesser and Coleman gives rise to several observations. First, it is unlikely that Coleman really intends, by his standard of "equal effects," to imply uniformity in pattern. While the difficulty in measuring equality would be significantly compounded

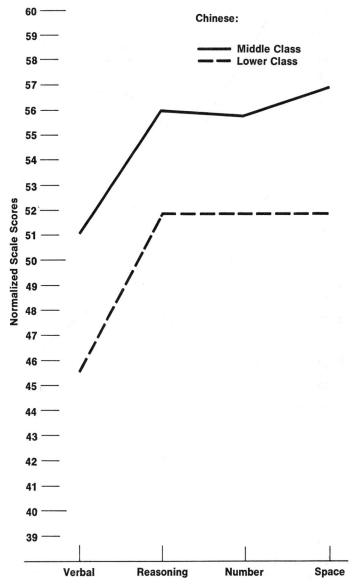

Fig. 1. Patterns of Normalized Mental-Ability Scores for
Middle- and Lower-Class Chinese Children.

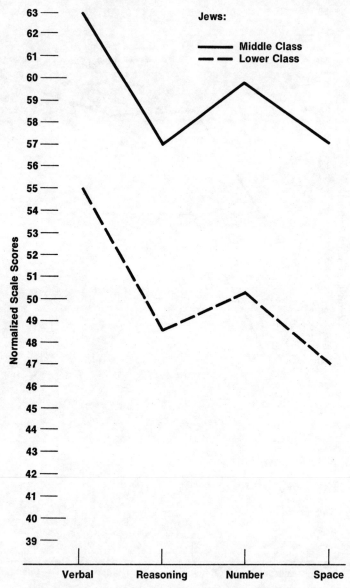

Fig. 2. Patterns of Normalized Mental-Ability Scores for Middle- and Lower-Class Jewish Children.

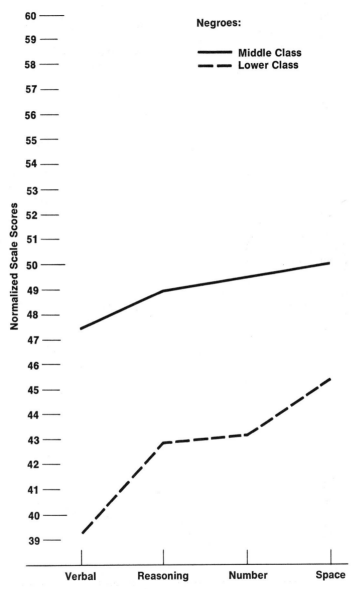

Fig. 3. Patterns of Normalized Mental-Ability Scores for
Middle- and Lower-Class Negro Children.

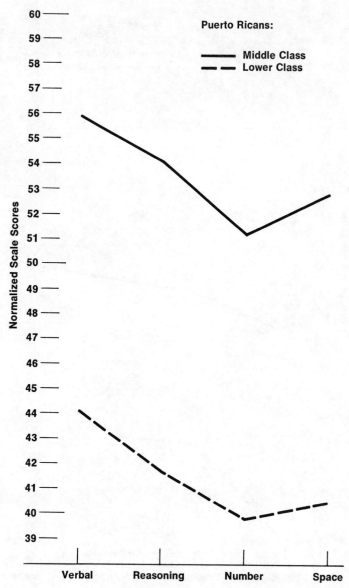

Fig. 4. Patterns of Normalized Mental-Ability Scores for Middle- and Lower-Class Puerto Rican Children.

were equivalent abilities in different areas judged adequate to meet the standard of equality, even a minimal respect for cultural diversity would appear to require that the difficulty be faced and a plural standard developed.

Second: Stodolsky and Lesser provide an example of "benign difference" in learning patterns. Their evidence indicates that Chinese children do best in space conceptualization, and are weakest in verbal ability, while Jewish children are strongest in verbal ability and weakest in space conceptualization.[25] If the schools were to encourage the special strengths of each, the authors point out, we might produce proportionally more Chinese than Jewish architects and engineers, and proportionally more Jewish than Chinese authors and lawyers. This result, though it is hardly uniform, is as surely not destructive, as Stodolsky and Lesser emphasize. But it is not difficult to imagine some differences in pattern which would not have such benign results. Society values both architects and lawyers; society does not hold all occupational choices in equally high regard, nor does it reward their practitioners equally well. Is it not likely that the distinctive patterns of a particular group might give it a special advantage in occupations which are, rightly or wrongly, held in low esteem, and are not well rewarded? The best example is probably a group distinguished in manual dexterity. We may argue that distinction in related occupations should be rewarded equally with distinction in other fields, but it is perfectly clear that it is not now so rewarded. From this illustration, we learn something of the bounds of pluralism in education. So long as the society values and rewards certain skills more than it does others, and so long as groups differ in their ability to acquire such skills, the schools will be trapped: if they promote group strengths, they also promote unequal ability to enjoy respect and income. If they adopt the societal values, and emphasize only those skills which command respect and income, some groups will consistently outperform others, and, once again, inequality will result. In either case, the burden of blame for continuing inequality in income falls centrally on the society, and not on the schools, which are helpless to overcome the societal definitions.

Third: Coleman holds social class integration necessary, since poor children do better in classrooms with middle-class children. But we have now seen that not all middle-class children have the same learning strengths and weaknesses. Insofar as many middle-class schools remain ethnically homogeneous, or, at least, are dominated by members of a single ethnic group, moving poor children from other ethnic groups into such schools would not only improve the achievement of the poor (Coleman) but would also impose on the learning pattern of the poor a different pattern, that of the dominant ethnic group (Stodolsky and Lesser). In passing, we should note that this might impede, rather than increase, educational achievement, since children might be slow to adjust to the change in pattern. But even if achievement were to increase, the obvious question is whether the price required is fair. Some might argue that there is no intrinsic value in the distinctive learning pattern of the group, and that there is, therefore, no cause to lament its disruption. Others, more moderate, might argue simply that between the goal of educational achievement which might lead to equality, and the goal of cultural pluralism, the former is the more compelling. But those who endorse both high achievement and pluralism are placed in an uncomfortable position by the demand for social-class integration, unless that demand is restricted to members of the same ethnic groupings. Since, as we have noted, there are insufficient numbers of middle-class Negroes to provide all poor Negroes with the opportunity to attend black class-integrated schools, social-class integration for black children necessarily points to racial integration as well. Thus, if we accept both bodies of data, we must conclude that Negro learning patterns are to be displaced, and to be displaced in a random way at that; whatever the dominant ethnic group in a particular school which Negroes attend, it is their pattern which Negroes will have to accept. This seems an especially brutal doctrine, insisting that black equality depends on an end to black distinctiveness. It also provides us with some confirmation of what was described in the second chapter as the "liberal perception" on the issue of race. There, we made the point that the underlying theory of integration depends on a rejection of particularism; here, we see that the behavioral implications of integration point in quite the same direction.*

Fourth, and most important: Stodolsky and Lesser themselves agree that "at least for basic skills (e.g., literacy) the achievement of equal levels by all children is desirable."[26] If the Coleman standard for equality were to be limited to such "basic" skills, the dispute might be settled. But here, Stodolsky and Lesser appear to contradict themselves. Literacy, for example, may be highly related to verbal ability. Jews, as we have seen, outperform other groups in verbal ability. Hence, if literacy is measured as an open-ended ability, Jews might set a standard that would be both difficult, and, in some sense, "unnecessary" for others to attain. The societal concern, aside from equality, is not, in the first instance, in making its citizens as literate as possible, but rather in ensuring that everyone achieves a minimum proficiency. Our concern, in other words, is not with the ceiling, a level which only some groups may approach, but with the floor. If the special abilities of a particular group permit it to rise above the needed floor in one area or another, there does not seem to be any intrinsic reason why that circumstance should result in an upward shift in the general standard.

Hence the mean performance of all groups may provide a flawed standard for measuring equality. But the fact is that if we accept the notion of a minimum floor, we depart from the conventional understanding of educational equality.

---

* But it may be argued that social pluralism does not depend on pluralism in education. Instead, one might contend, the family and community can be depended on to preserve difference, while the task of the school is to bring the diverse social groups together. This is an important position, which we take up in Chapter Five.

For the floor can be defined independently of the behavior of groups, according to some a priori statement regarding the requirements of the good life. It clearly cannot be defined by the behavior of that group which does best, for then it is no longer a floor, but a ceiling. Using the concept of floor, we are required to revise the Coleman standard as follows: "Some groups are disabled educationally by the environment. The schools should be required, with respect to those skills deemed essential by society, to insure that all children, including the disabled, achieve that level of competence considered minimally necessary in each of the named skills." Beyond that level, we would expect that each group would develop a distinctive pattern of performance; as among such patterns, the society makes no preferential judgments.

But if such a revision is plausible, the educational argument for integration will have to be re-examined. We do not know how those groups which are, by current standards, defined as educational failures, would fare were they guided by a different standard, and encouraged, beyond that standard, to pursue the areas of their students' strengths. And if we accept the revised statement, what happens to the concept of "gap"? For if our primary concern is with minimally adequate performance, according to an a priori standard—or, indeed, any standard that is independent of the behavior of groups—then the fact that some groups do better than others is no longer the focus of attention. Our only concern with intergroup comparisons arises when some meet, or exceed, the minimal standard, while others do not—in which case it is still the gap between the underachieving group and the minimum, rather than between it and some other group, that is the source of our concern.

All of which leaves the debate over the *educational* consequences of community control essentially where it started. Some evidence supports the position that racial integration is required in order to achieve equality, while other evidence shows that racial integration has overtones of cultural imperialism. Some arguments imply that the "gap" is our major problem, while other arguments insist that we should not be concerned with comparisons among groups, but only with the adequacy of performance relative to a fixed minimal standard. In short, our choices here cannot be made, given the present state of theoretical consensus and empirical evidence, on the basis of data alone; our choices are between competing values, and should be so regarded.

There are several other considerations, however, which have been introduced by participants in the debate, and which, while not directly related to educational consequences, deserve attention. We may recall, for example, the argument introduced in the preceding chapter regarding legitimacy. If it is true that in the present climate, many black parents have withdrawn their confidence in the public school system, it can be argued that whatever steps are required to restore confidence should be taken, since there can be no serious educational improvement in the absence of confidence. From this proposition, a number of commentators have moved directly to an endorsement of community control. The connection is not, however, entirely clear. While it may well be true that communities some of whose members now press for community control would regard the schools as legitimate were such control established, it can also be argued that it is chiefly the crisis in integration which has eroded the perceived legitimacy of the school system. Were the promise of integration fulfilled, Negro performance would improve, and confidence would be restored. Further, a sudden restoration of confidence, and a shift to community control, would provide only a necessary condition for educational improvement. In the end, it is only through continuing effectiveness that the school system can expect to be regarded as legitimate. If it were true that effectiveness could not be achieved in segregated schools, the temporary victory of community control would prove hollow, indeed, and Negro parents would be still more disillusioned than they are today, since the schools themselves would be no better for the victory. In this view, while it may be politic in the short run to concede community control to those who seek it, it might have disastrous long-range consequences; at best, it would prove a deception to people genuinely aggrieved. Better, then, to deal with the crisis in legitimacy by attacking its roots—the failure in effectiveness; disregard the passions of the moment, and do whatever is necessary to increase effectiveness.

But our difficulty is threefold. First, we cannot be sure how effectiveness is most readily attainable. To say "effectiveness" does not yet say whether integration or compensation or community control or some other reform, or combination of reforms, is the best approach. Second, a strong case can be made for the view that matters have deteriorated so, at least in a number of cities, that the symptom must be dealt with before the disease can be addressed. The climate of hostility and violence is intense, and even if community control is no more than a temporary palliative, the school system can no longer in fairness ask Negroes to postpone their gratification while some new effort at increased effectiveness is mounted. Such efforts are no longer credible to many people, and lacking credibility, they cannot succeed. In short, the passions of the moment will overwhelm the effort. Third, if for effectiveness we require integration, a la Coleman, then we are brought up short once again by the *Realpolitik* of integration. Short of a firm national commitment to full integration, progress towards integration will continue to be sluggish. And even with the commitment, demography will intervene, unless there is a dramatic shift away from locally bounded school districts and towards metropolitan districts. Would not such a shift, even if accepted by whites, be widely interpreted by blacks as yet another effort by the "white power structure" to deprive them of their long awaited chance to exercise control over their own communities?

A different consideration is introduced by some proponents of community schools, who hold that "forced" integration is, in its own way, as stigmatizing as *de facto* segregation. We have reviewed this position in an earlier chapter, and it is easily summarized: to insist that black children, when poor, must, for their educational salvation, attend schools that are predominantly white, is to suggest that blacks are, in some significant way, inferior to whites. All the modifying clauses, which emphasize environmental disability or poverty rather than race, are almost certain to be obscured.

This point may be illustrated with an example from a different, but related, area. A civil rights group interested in desegregating housing recently solicited signatures to a "Personal Housing Action Pledge." Among several things signers were asked to commit themselves to was the following:

> When I change my residence, I will refuse to let myself be used to perpetuate segregation but will make my own choices, and specifically, if white, I will *actively seek* housing away from areas of white concentration, preferably on a block where some black people live. If black, I will *actively seek* housing away from areas of black concentration, preferably on a block where black people do not live. [Italics in original.]

It can easily be argued that only by such personal action will the debilitating pattern of racial segregation in America be ended. Surely, liberal perspectives on the issue of race would support the sentiments of the pledge. But the necessary assumption of the pledge, and, in particular, of the promise of black people to seek housing on blocks where other blacks do not live, is that there is no reason for black people to seek each other out, that there are no special ties which bind black people to one another. Suppose, for the moment, that such a pledge were elicited, and similar assumptions thereby made, about Chinese, or Jews. Or, suppose that Chinese or Jews were forbidden to attend schools whose students were predominantly Chinese or Jewish. At the very minimum, one must recognize that such a policy, even if it were perceived as leading, in the end, to a nobler world, would create very serious resentments among the groups affected.

It is not that segregation is good and integration bad, but that legal recognition of the special status of the Negro may have negative overtones, whether the purpose is to keep him apart or to mix him in with others. In both cases, the right of Negroes to free association is limited.

The answer, of course, is that there is an equally powerful limitation on free association already, through *de facto* segregation, through ghettoization and the rest. As between restrictions on free association, a restriction which promotes interracial relationships is to be preferred to one which prohibits them. But advocates of community control will ask —and their question cannot be casually dismissed—whether, indeed, the best that American society has to offer blacks is a choice between two different forms of restriction. It may, as a matter of general public policy, be thought wise, or right, to forbid segregation, whatever its source. But it cannot seriously be suggested that a policy which is beneficent for the society as a whole is necessarily equally beneficent for all the individuals in that society. Some blacks, presumably, if given a genuinely free choice, would prefer to associate primarily with other blacks. The issue before society is not with whom people choose to associate, but whether they in fact have a free choice. In this context, integration becomes a tactical problem, and not an end in itself; given the tawdry history of race relations in America, is integration (by law) required as a step on the way to free choice, or are there other ways in which free choice can be as easily, or more easily, reached?

This point needs to be emphasized before we move on, since it is always tempting to convert tactic into strategy, especially when the tactic itself proves difficult to accomplish. Whether for that reason, or because, as we suggested in an earlier chapter, some people who are themselves committed to a groupless society insist that their commitment be applied to others, integration is frequently viewed as a substantive social benefit. Yet, if freedom for Negroes means anything at all, it has to mean that Negroes themselves may choose how important their group affiliation shall be. It is painfully clear that no such choice is possible today; it may be the case that in order to make it possible at some future time, integration must be mandated. But "it may be the case" is a fragile foundation for public policy.

Public Policy and Educational Equality

The implication of the last sentence would seem to be that Negroes themselves ought to be allowed to choose the educational system they prefer. That, however, overstates the case. Wherever possible, the state should defer to the wishes of the individual or the group. But the limits of possibility are provided by the concept of the "general welfare." When the desires of groups do not carry implications beyond the boundaries of the group, it can fairly be said that the good of all is enhanced by promoting the good of each, as each defines that good for itself. But most important social issues have significant spillover effects, and few more significant than public education. From general socialization to literacy to citizenship, the state depends critically on the schools; while its stake in the schools may at times be exaggerated, what happens in the schools is surely of public moment, and hence of public concern.

In extreme cases, this point is perfectly clear. The state both mandates that certain things shall be taught in the schools and proscribes other things. And, if the schools did not themselves acknowledge responsibility for teaching many of the things they try to teach, governmental controls would doubtless be enlarged. The notion of a common curriculum, at least in its basic parts, is deeply embedded in American educational philosophy and practice.

But there are subtler kinds of issues than departures from the core curriculum, and it is in dealing with such issues that the scope and limits of public policy become more difficult to define. Let us imagine, for example, a suburban school district in a city of, say, fifty thousand, including a mix of working class and affluent families. The several elementary schools have largely homogeneous student bodies, since neighborhoods within the city are fairly well-defined, and follow income lines. The school system has a reputation for excellence, but, like most systems, it is always short of funds, and cannot do quite what it would like to do. Imagine, further, that one of the things it cannot do is reduce the teacher-pupil ratio below its present level. Now, suppose that a group of affluent parents approaches the principal of the school in its neighborhood and offers to provide funds to hire a new teacher for a particularly overcrowded grade. From one perspective, this might be thought a perfectly laudable example of civic-minded voluntarism. Would we not applaud the working-class parents had they volunteered to provide lunch-room supervisors in order to free teachers to spend more time in the classroom? But, while our affluent parents might be motivated by the highest purposes, it is not at all clear that the public interest is well-served by their offer. It might well be, for example, that a more critical need exists in another school, and that if a new sum of money is to be made available, it should, "properly," be allocated elsewhere. "Properly," in this context, means according to the judgment of responsible officials concerning the needs of the system. If there are parents in the city who are both able and willing to provide more support for education, the appropriate mechanism for handling the transaction would appear to be taxation, or, if via donation, then a donation to the system for use as it sees fit. Only thus can the moneys be allocated for the "general welfare." In short, what may be good for one group within the community may not be good for the community, whether because it pre-empts the authority of those charged with policy-making responsibility or because it destroys the possibility of systemic equity.

Similarly, it is not possible to rest the case for community control with the assertion that Negroes are entitled to determine the educational guidelines for their own communities. There may be a presumption in favor of permitting as much communal self-determination as possible, but such a presumption would have to meet at least two tests: first, it would have to be shown that the divestiture of policy-making power from the general educational authority would not have detrimental consequences for the rest of the community. Second, those Negroes who do not choose, for whatever reason, to identify themselves with the Negro community, would have to be provided for. As to the first of these considerations, the current climate is not at all encouraging. Too often, the demand for community control appears to be joined with somewhat bizarre statements regarding what should be taught in those schools, statements which the general society cannot be expected to accept, much less welcome, and which discredit the seriousness of the argument. As to the second, it is still difficult to know how many parents are genuinely committed to community control, and how many remain skeptical, if not hostile, to it. Since the connection between the two is not, at this stage, demonstrably necessary, the minimal requirements of freedom point to a school structure that would permit parents to opt out of the community controlled school if they so chose.

The provision of options is warranted also by the fears expressed in some quarters that community controlled schools might impose a kind of minority tyranny on the passive majority. Those who express this fear argue that operationally, "community" must be defined as "that group of residents which successfully imposes its programs on all the children of the district."[27] We have already noted that, vis-à-vis the black community, the present situation is hardly more attractive, since it, too, involves domination by a minority, and an alien minority at that. But, to the extent that all forms of domination should be excised, any structural reform should permit some measure of choice.

Let us attempt a more precise definition of the public policy considerations which bear on the community control controversy, and in particular on the controversy between the integrationists and the communalists. In an earlier chapter, we suggested that genuine pluralism is not to be understood merely as diversity, but rather as a structured diversity, with elements of both group cohesion and group interaction. Simple interaction, without anchor points, leads to mass society with its associated ailments. And simple cohesion, without mobility, leads to a caste society. From this simple paradigm, it is possible to derive several operational principles. Chief among them is the need for an educational system that provides for balance between the small community and the larger society. The connection between the general social structure and the structure of the educational system may not be obvious, so it is best to make it explicit:

Our first premise is that structural pluralism is a desirable goal for the American polity. Next, we observe that pluralism is an unsteady state, since it involves a continuing tension between the pull towards cohesion and the requirement for interaction. Accordingly, we may find that some people emphasize the one and some the other. We may imagine a continuum from pure cohesion to pure interaction, with a mid-point that expresses the joining of the two; we cannot automatically conclude that all people "should" be somewhere near the mid-point. The needed distribution may be a normal curve, but it may also be a nearly flat line, with only a slight peaking in the middle. As Berelson notes, the health of the collectivity is an aggregate function, and does not depend on each person reflecting the same characteristics.[28]

We know, however, that those closest to the ends of the continuum will not be able to exercise genuine free choice in setting their own life styles. Those who are deeply bound up in the small community may develop blinders which inhibit interaction, or such idiosyncratic characteristics that others, of alien communities, will shun them. Similarly, those who are most free-floating may be characterologically incapable of active participation in more anchored communal styles. If we seek to maximize choice, it is reasonable to try to provide all citizens with some direct experience with the different modalities. And one plausible place to provide such experience is the school system.

From the viewpoint of society at large, it might be sufficient to provide a dual school system, one component heavily based in the community, one on more universal foundations. From the viewpoint of the individual, it appears desirable to provide exposure to both. Hence one can imagine a school system which is explicit, but not monolithic, about its value orientations, and in which all children, at various times, are involved with the major alternative orientations.

We examine such possibilities more carefully in the next chapter. For the moment, the critical point is the triple linkage between public policy considerations, school system structures, and educational benefits. For it now becomes clear that the structure of the school system may have educational implications every bit as significant as the specific curricular content. What gets taught in the classroom, and even how it gets taught, are aspects of schooling, but only aspects. The mood and temper of the school, the patterns of authority, and the value commitments the school reflects, are another aspect. We have no empirical evidence that would permit us to say which is the more important aspect, but inasmuch as one major responsibility of the schools is the socialization of the young, it is not unreasonable to suppose that the extracurricular environment, with all the value-oriented cues that it emits, is of great consequence.

If, then, we ask to know the likely educational implications of community control, we are best advised to include in our assessment those aspects of education that are least tied to curriculum, since it is there that major changes can be anticipated. If we do so, we learn that there are positive values associated with community control, but that those values are not the only values the polity promotes, or tries to be about. Perhaps, then, the task of the schools is not to opt decisively for community-oriented values, but rather to reflect more accurately the alternative orientations of the society and polity, and, even more, the continuing effort to join the two central orientations in creative tension.

School and Community

We have suggested that the formal curriculum is only an aspect of education, a suggestion frequently made but rarely acted upon. Without entering into a detailed discussion of the special responsibilities of the school within a comprehensive educational strategy, one point merits special attention. Insofar as cohesive communities in the United States are interested in providing a communally oriented education for their children, many are able to do so, and have traditionally done so, through voluntary (i.e., nonpublic) devices. The most notable examples, of course, are the Catholic parochial schools, the afternoon private schools maintained by several ethnic groups, including the Jews, the Greeks, and the Chinese, and programs of released time for religious instruction which exist in many communities. Some groups turn the public schools to communal purposes, a condition especially prevalent where there is substantial ethnic homogeneity in a particular region, where both the managers of the system and its constituents share a communal orientation. And some people, those who feel no special kinship to "private" communities, find the state system perfectly adequate.

Now, however, a number of black people are insisting that the public schools of the state be turned to communal purposes. Indeed, their position goes beyond education, for, increasingly, there is talk not only of control over curriculum, but also over contracts, construction, and the like. Such a proposal involves an implicit rejection of two alternative models for pursuing community; both the school maintained by the community itself and the heterogeneous state school are, apparently, judged inadequate or unfeasible. The difficulty in generating enthusiasm for the proposal derives from the fact that the state system has never explicitly endorsed communal purposes; on the contrary, wherever it has been forced to make an explicit statement, it has denied those purposes.

Yet it is true that locally oriented state schools, in the South, in rural areas, in suburbs, and even in large cities, do serve parochial as well as secular ends, in what might well be termed *de facto* community control. Nor is this a recent phenomenon. Leonard Covello led a major effort to tie New York City schools more closely to their communities in the early decades of this century, and met with substantial success.[29] Although he began his work with, and derived his insights from, the Italian group—his own—he later succeeded in transferring the general theoretical model to his work with Puerto Rican and other ethnic groups. That, however, appears a rare exception, for, in general, the leitmotiv of the community finds authentic expression in the school only when the teachers and administrators are themselves part of the community.

In this connection, a major inhibition in pursuing communal understandings in schools, even where the ethnic backgrounds of students and teachers are similar, may be that many teachers, especially in major urban centers, are second-generation, upwardly mobile people. As such, they are often caught up in an effort to escape their own community of origin, viewing their task as freeing their students from the negative qualities of the group they themselves remain somewhat embarrassed by.[30] Insofar as this is so, it is not enough to match the ethnicity of the teacher to that of his students; indeed, such matching may be less important than recruitment of teachers who are sympathetic to the authenticity of the ethnic culture they deal with.

In brief, many Americans seek to expose their children to an essentially private (particular, parochial) curriculum as well as to the conventional public curriculum. Those who do not are more or less adequately served by the state schools, which emphasize the public curriculum. Those who do are often in a position to create special institutions which concentrate on the private curriculum, or so to influence the state schools as to insure that they will have both public and private components. But blacks are too poor to create their own schools, and too exploited, educationally, to turn the public schools to private purpose; what they seek, therefore, is *de jure* community control.

We may introduce here a historical hypotheses that aids our understanding. In an earlier era, the tension between the educational purposes of the state and those of the community was not particularly problematic, since most communities were fairly confident of their ability to control extraschool education. The community ethic was substantially more defined than it has come to be of late, and competition from noncontrollable media of communications was quite limited. Now, however, such competition poses a serious threat to the ability of any parochial community to transmit its own understandings, and the understandings themselves are far less certain. Those who seek to impart what remains of the communal ethic to the young must devote time and energy to the task, where before "the environment" could be trusted to do the job. What is needed now, as a replacement for the folk tradition, is an institutional address. And if one must either build a new institution or convert an old one, is it not easier to try to convert the old one, especially when (a) one lacks the resources to build a new one, and (b) the old one, in any case, is failing to do the job for which it was originally intended?

The difficulty here is that the original job still needs doing. Even were blacks able to find a means, within the schools or without, for satisfying their communal needs, that would not solve the problem of black failure in the public sector. Some theorists and practitioners have suggested that a more relevant (read, "communally-oriented") curriculum would lead to greater interest, hence to higher achievement, hence, finally, to better performance across the board, and this may be so.[31] We simply do not know—nor will we ever be in a position to know unless there is a serious attempt to test the theory.

Critics of community control, reflecting dispositions discussed throughout these pages, often fear that to permit the introduction of private curricula into public schools would politicize those schools, converting the classroom into a caucus, converting pedagogy into proselytization. They have in mind, for example, sentiments such as those expressed in a recent article by a leading practitioner of community-oriented education:[32]

> Let me first state two things that a Black school does not do: it does not deprecate "White culture"; it does not create Black myths.[33]
>
> The Black school's first task is to destroy White myths. The task of exposing White myths for what they are is, superficially, an easy one.[34]
>
> The Black family must be extended to include all Black folks—the Uncle Tom (if there is such a character), the militant, the nationalist, the culturalist, the NAACP-er, the integrationist. All Blacks must be brought into the extended Black family.[35]
>
> My greatest fear is that many Blacks will be deluded into believing that they have achieved "middle-class status" and may be caught in the crossfire as the oppressed try to eliminate their oppressors. All *Black Folk* are too beautiful to be so sacrificed.[36]

The philosophy represented in these citations may or may not be thought responsible; it is clear, however, that the stated disclaimer regarding deprecating white culture and creating black myths is belied in the subsequent argument. All cultures are in part mythological, and, if the black school promotes black culture, it necessarily promotes black mythology as well. Similarly, to replace white myths implies a deprecation of white culture. The article proposes, for example, that the story of Custer's last stand be reoriented, so that Sitting Bull emerges as the hero.[37] That might well be the honest thing to do; if so, honesty involves a reformation of white culture, and, therefore, a deprecation of present white understandings.

Up to a point, such reformations are perfectly plausible, and would elicit widespread support. But we are in need not only of a black culture and a white culture, but also an American culture. Perhaps, in the past, the national culture, necessarily informed centrally by white myths, has received disproportionate attention, and parochial myths, including those central to black culture, have suffered neglect. Nonetheless, the nation has a substantial interest in insuring that if now, at long last, it seeks to redress the imbalance, and to permit greater scope to the expression of private understandings, the core ingredients of the national mythology are not thereby sacrificed. This requires of the nation that it define more precisely what is the core, and what the periphery; we may be able to survive the loss of General Custer, but Abraham Lincoln may be an entirely different matter. Some symbols, or myths, or understandings, need to survive the effort at pluralizing the society, and state-supported schools must be expected to honor them. The effort, after all, is to pluralize, not to Balkanize.

Which brings us once again to the question of balance, and to our final chapter.

CHAPTER FIVE

SOCIAL ARRANGEMENTS AND THE SCHOOLS

THE IMMEDIATE cause of the demand for community control of the schools is the massive failure of the public schools to do the job that has traditionally been assigned them: teaching all students the skills society considers basic. "All" is, of course, something of an exaggeration; severely handicapped students have been excepted from the mandate. But when large groups in the society fail to perform adequately, it will simply not do to say that those groups are handicapped, and thereby to exculpate the schools. Society may be able to afford the failure of the randomly handicapped, even if their number is large; it cannot afford the systematic failure of specific groups of children.

The evident failure of the schools to meet their responsibilities is not, however, the sole justification for community control. Indeed, were the only issue at stake the relatively straightforward one of educational attainment, traditionally measured, it is not clear that any serious structural revision of the schools would be required. New curricula, new teaching techniques, new facilities, new ways of composing the student body—all these and more are compatible with public education as it is structured today, and might be adequate to do the job. What makes community control a special kind of demand, essentially different from other proposed educational reforms, is that it relates to a variety of issues that go beyond the question of educational attainment.

As we have seen, these issues include such matters as legitimacy, pluralism, and so on. The most important, and the most comprehensive, is the issue of community itself, of the ways in which Americans understand and deal with the impulse to fraternity. Because that is so, the demand for community control is also a demand that we redefine the mission of public education, and not limit our efforts merely to improving the performance of the schools. For so long as our efforts are so limited, the schools will continue to be about what they have been about, more successfully or less, over the years, which is to say, they will continue to neglect what now appears to be a profound effort to raise fundamental questions regarding educational philosophy and societal ideology.

The Uses of Ethnicity: The Polity

It is not hard to make the case for an increase in fraternity in America. That case has been made a thousand times over, and almost everyone is likely to find that it has been argued in ways congenial to his own special focus. But when we come to apply the general argument to the specific problem of public education, we encounter at least three problems. First, it is not obvious that the schools are an appropriate locus for the pursuit of fraternity. Second, even if it is decided that society would benefit from schools more oriented to fraternity, it is not obvious that race and ethnicity are proper bases for the development of fraternity. Perhaps all that is needed is an increase in attention to affective education. And third, if it is a balance between fraternity and other values that we seek, then we need to know how much the turn towards fraternity involves a turn away from other values, and how, if at all, we can calibrate the movement.

The first two questions are intertwined, for a decision on the wisdom of opening the schools to greater fraternity may depend on our understanding of the sources of fraternity. No threat to education may be perceived if our concern is merely with the ways in which students, however selected, relate to one another. If, however, we are speaking of that special kind of relationship which assumes selected student bodies, whose relationships precede the school setting and go beyond it, quite another conclusion may be warranted. As we have seen, to permit fraternity to be defined in racial and ethnic terms threatens not only traditional understandings of the purposes of public education, but also, and perhaps more fundamentally, traditional perceptions of the proper bases of association in a heterogeneous democratic society. According to those perceptions, groups within the society may be tolerated, perhaps even encouraged, but only if they are based on instrumental interests rather than organic relationships; organic groups threaten the primacy of the state's claim on the citizen's loyalty.

We have reviewed some of the general reasons for the deep-seated fears concerning the dangers of endorsing ethnicity and race as benign bases for association. The case against ethnicity can be argued in historical terms, resting primarily on the frequency with which ethnicity has fostered ethnocentricity. It can be argued in normative terms, emphasizing the degree to which permitting small fraternities within the family of man is likely to impede the advent of the ultimate fraternity, the brotherhood of all mankind. And it can be argued in terms of the American experience. Has not the very purpose of the nation been to take "the tired," "the poor," "the huddled masses," "the wretched refuse" of Europe's "teeming shore," and to convert them into Americans? Thus, Israel Zangwill:

> America is God's Crucible, the great Melting Pot where all the races of Europe are melting and reforming! Here you stand, good folk, think I, when I see them at Ellis Island, here you stand in your fifty groups with your fifty languages and histories, and your fifty blood hatreds and rivalries, but you won't be long like that brothers, for these are the fires of God you've come to—these are the fires of God. A fig for your feuds and vendettas!

German and Frenchman, Irishman and Englishman, Jews and Russians—into the crucible with you all! God is making the American.[1]

Nor was Zangwill's somewhat purple prose exceptional; it was echoed, before and after, by men of affairs as well as letters. Jefferson had been worried about immigration, fearing that the immigrants would "infuse into (legislation) their spirit, warp and bias its directions, and render it a heterogeneous, incoherent, distracted mass."[2] John Quincy Adams held that new immigrants "must cast off the European skin, never to resume it. They must look forward to their posterity rather than backward to their ancestors."[3] And Woodrow Wilson believed that "A man who thinks of himself as belonging to a particular national group has not yet become an American."[4]

These citations suggest that still another source of the pursuit of a uniform morality and a unitary ethic has been the effort by certain groups to rationalize their own social position. In the case of traditional elites, Americanization meant what Milton Gordon calls "Anglo-conformity," an attempt to make the culture of a single group the dominant, if not exclusive, culture for the entire nation.[5] The battle was not against tradition, but against alien tradition. In the case of liberal intellectuals, themselves long cut off from folk society, the purposes were somewhat different; tradition itself was the enemy.

It is curious that a developing polity which placed so much stress on individual liberty, and expressed so much suspicion of government, should at the same time have so vehemently insisted on the right of the state to near-exclusive claim on the loyalties of its citizens. We can, after all, imagine a polity which makes only limited claims on the affections and loyalties of its citizens, permitting them to maintain and develop other affections and other loyalties as well. Perhaps the artificial beginnings of the American nation and America's self-consciousness about its special, almost holy, mission help to explain the unusual emphasis the nation places on its unifying symbols.[6] In the historic countries of Europe, the society antedated the polity; civil government could be seen as a convenient way for the society to handle certain kinds of problems. In the United States, a rather different perspective developed out of the rapid changes in the composition and character of the society. If unity was required, it had to come from the State, and be consciously pursued; it could not, as it was in Europe, be assumed.

Thus there did not develop, in this country, a "polity of limited liability," a polity which, under normal circumstances, can afford its citizens great latitude in defining their networks of commitment. Separatism is a threat not only to the American "arrangement"; it is a threat to the American purpose, to the very justification for the American experiment. Hence it is profoundly subversive.

And yet, "the point about the melting pot is that it did not happen."[7] For some people, for some groups, perhaps, but not nearly so comprehensively as Zangwill and others had wished. And the nation, more or less, has thrived nonetheless. This suggests that the ethnic bond is more important to people, and less subversive to the nation, than theoreticians had supposed.

That it is more important to people than had been predicted, or hoped, raises the question of the functions which ethnic identity serves in American society. Diverse explanations may be, and have been, offered. Some see in the survival of ethnicity the reflection of a deep, almost primeval urge, others a specific result of distinctive group experiences in this country. Surely, the very lack of traditional sources for self-location in the American social landscape led many people to search for anchor points in their own past. Without caste, without the extended family, without identification of self with a specific place, yet with a need to order oneself in relation to others, a need not fully satisfied by instrumental interest groups, the ethnic group becomes a plausible starting point—all the more so when ethnicity and religious affiliation overlap substantially.

More important to the individual, less subversive to the nation. How could the social censors who had foretold national disaster unless the ethnic instinct were extirpated have been so wrong? Apparently the mistake was to assume that ethnicity, once allowed, would overwhelm; at the very least, the ethnic tie would leave no room for the development of the needed tie to polyethnic America; at most, the colliding ethnics would fragment America. Left out of the analysis was a recognition of the fact that the fluidity of America, itself a chief source of the urge to ethnic identification, was also an antidote to that identification. Not only the ethic of individualism, but also the spatial and social mobility of the new nation, and, centrally, the impossibility of locating definitively the boundaries of the ethnic group, made the development of genuinely organic communities impossible. What distinguished the American experience was that membership in the quasi-organic ethnic was still, in large measure, voluntary, not predetermined. And the intrusion of symbols and ideas and people from outside the group simply could not be prevented. The fundamentally voluntary quality of ethnicity in America was unprecedented, and, therefore, a source of significant confusion.

Ethnic leaders themselves abetted the confusion. Their task, as they saw it, was to defend against alien incursions. Committed as they were, whether out of ideology or out of more personalized motive, to the survival of the ethnic group, they were bound to argue that the group had intrinsic merit, that its survival was a valuable goal, and not merely a helpful means to its members. Since this meant that the ethnic group was to endure indefinitely into the future, and not merely serve proximate needs in a tumultuous present, consideration of its functional utility was diverted, replaced by debate over its legitimacy. Neither ethnic leaders nor social theoreticians, distracted by ideological debate—the one insisting that the group was its own justification, the other that America could not imperil its future by accepting the group —fully understood the ways in which people were using ethnic groups in America, and the changes in the meanings of ethnicity and ethnic identification that were unfolding as a result. For most people, ethnicity had not become a way of life, nor the ethnic group its own justification; rather, the group had become a convenient launching point for the journey into a larger America, and a refuge from that journey when respite was wanted.

Some people, of course, sought to live the greater part of their lives within the confines of the group. And some groups —in particular, those where ethnic and religious identity reinforced each other—came to be invested with eschatological purposes. But even those people who were most deeply involved with their ethnic group took pride in their brothers who had "made it" in the larger America, and hoped that their own children, though loyal to the group, would also move beyond its pale. Early social commentators had imagined that the preservation of ethnic identity would impede the development of American identity; they neglected the capacity of almost every ethnic group to graft onto its own traditions and understandings the core beliefs of the American ideology, a process made necessary if, indeed, the ethnic group was to serve as launching pad. They neglected, further, the nonideological origins of ethnicity, preferring instead to take the ideological rationales put forward by ethnic leaders at face value. But most ethnic groups offered their members a home, and a set of traditions, oriented mostly around the great crises of a person's life—birth, marriage, and death. They rarely spoke to the question of belief. Ethnic identity was an exercise more in integration and intimacy than in ideology and belief. And so, in large measure, it has remained, except where there has taken place a direct collision between the ethnic identity and the American purpose— say, for example, the dilemma of German-Americans during the Great Wars.

But if it is true that American forms of ethnic identification have tended, on the whole, to be benign, and have not subverted loyalties to larger units, such as the nation itself, the interests of the polity may be best served by taking the same view of ethnic identification the polity takes of religious identification—distant, but supportive. On the basis of the American experience, in short, the answer to the question of whether ethnicity is a proper basis for fraternal association is affirmative. Propriety, according to American doctrine, is a matter for individual determination. The burden of proof that the choice of the individual is damaging to the society is with the society, and an argument based on a specific social philosophy, whether derived from the Enlightenment or from any other partial perspective, ignorant of the special meanings of ethnicity in America, cannot be thought adequate to fulfill that burden.

The Uses of Ethnicity: The Individual

The polity does have an additional concern, and that is whether individuals themselves are trapped by the ethnic group, unable, even if they wish it, to break the historic ties and to forge some new identity for themselves. Religion, after all, is a matter (formally) of belief, not of birth; the individual is free, more or less, to convert to some other religious belief, or even to "convert" to no religion at all. But he cannot adopt ethnic origins at will; such origins are entirely ascribed, and the only choice available is how much they shall matter. So, Oscar Handlin:

> In a period in which the isolated individual must confront the immense powers of the state and of other massive organizations of the naked society, mediating institutions, such as those provided by the ethnic group, can still serve important functions. They can provide him with legitimate means by which he can assert his individuality if he wishes to do so. On the other hand, if these groups become rigid and fall into place among the other instruments by which the individual is con-

trolled and regulated, then they become assimilated to the other massive organizations that crush rather than liberate him.[8]

The author of the concept of "cultural pluralism," Horace Kallen, once spoke of America as a "nation of nations," a federation of ethnic groups living in harmony with one another.[9] Zangwill, who coined the term "melting pot," endorsed a rather different vision of America, an American that had been described by Henry Jackson Turner, chronicler of the frontier, as a "crucible," site of "a new product, which held the promise of world brotherhood."[10] Is it possible to imagine an America where either option is available, an America equally willing to accept people-as-individuals and people-as-groups? For it is the answer to that question that tells us the answer to the more fundamental question, whether, indeed, the individual is himself free to determine how much ethnicity shall matter. If the basic building blocks of America are individuals, as the vision of the melting pot suggests, ethnicity is deprecated; if the basic building blocks are groups, as Kallen and the cultural pluralists suggest, freedom is constrained. Only in an America where the individual is able to decide whether to strike his contract with the nation for himself, or as part of a group, can genuine pluralism—and genuine freedom—be realized.

The American ideological deck has surely been stacked in favor of the individual ethic. But the American experience is hardly unitary, and a steady counterpoint has emphasized the virtues of groupness. America has not been a nation of nations, nor, today, would most Americans accept the validity of Kallen's formulation as a goal. But neither has America been entirely a collection of random individuals, and many Americans continue to resist raw individualism as an appropriate aim. Instead, the American experience, in the main, has permitted each person to establish the character of his own relationship to the whole. There are several factors which have made this flexibility possible:

1. As Milton Gordon, in his very useful book, *Assimilation in American Life,* points out, we have had more structural pluralism than cultural pluralism in this country.[11] By this Gordon intends that ideological differences have been negligible, and value orientations quite similar, among the many groups; pluralism has not meant serious diversity in these spheres. Instead, it has been chiefly structural, marking off certain functional boundaries which define spheres of interaction, rather than belief. This, in turn, has made the persistence of groups tolerable, since, with rare exception, there has been little overlap between group identity and instrumental interests. Had such overlap existed, groups would have collided with each other far more often than they have.

2. Gordon's view is closely related to the fact that the national ideology has been integrated into the culture of the parochial groups. For as most groups were used by their members to fulfill personal needs rather than to promote ideological ends, they existed, as it were, in an ideological vacuum. The national ideology was not, therefore, required to compete against particular group ideologies; it could simply attach itself to the folkways.

This statement glosses over some of the strains which were, from time to time, involved in the process of immigrant acculturation in America. In the area of our own concern, for example, we find vehement reaction by Catholics to laws for compulsory education:

> The general principle upon which these laws are based is radically unsound, untrue, Atheistical. . . . It is, that the education of children is not the work of the Church, or of the Family, but that it is the work of the State. . . . Two consequences flow from this principle. . . . In the matter of education, the State is supreme over the Church and the Family. *Hence,* the State can and does exclude from the schools religious instruction. . . . The inevitable consequence is, that . . . the greater number of scholars must turn out to be Atheists, and accordingly the majority of non-Catholics are people of no religion. . . . The other consequence . . . leads the State to *adopt*

the child, to weaken the ties which bind it to the parent. So laws are made compelling children to attend the state schools, and forbidding the parents, if they be poor, to withdraw their little ones from the school. . . . The consequence of this policy is . . . universal disobedience on the part of children. . . . Our little boys scoff at their parents, call their fathers by the name of Old Man, Boss, or Governor. The mother is the Old Woman. The little boys smoke, drink, blaspheme, talk about fornication, and so far as they are physically able, commit it. Our little girls read novels . . . quarrel about their beaux, uphold Woman's Rights, and—. . . . We were a Boston school boy, and we speak of what we know.[12]

Yet religious particularism had special difficulties, not generally encountered by ethnic groups, since the very basis of religion is eschatological, hence also ideological, while most ethnic groups are organized around nostalgia. Hence it may not be entirely accidental that some of the European ethnic groups are among the most assiduously patriotic of all America's groups; though their group be hyphenated, their ideology is All American.

3. These two factors made the ethnic group able to coexist with the nation, since neither found it necessary to claim the total loyalty of the citizen. Alone, however, they could not guarantee free choice to the citizen, since, in an America of nationality groups, one's identity would necessarily be fixed at birth. It is important, therefore, to emphasize again that the ethnic group is only one style of American group life. Since the beginning, other kinds of associations have existed, and, especially in recent times, alternative groups have flourished. Substantial difficulties have been placed in the paths of those who sought to trade one ethnic identity for another; swarthy people, the Grosse Pointe realtors have told us, make bad Wasps. But few difficulties have awaited those who sought to move away from ethnicity, into communities resting on different bases. Middle managers and hippies,

academics and artists, have been able, where they wanted to, to slip away from the ethnic group. This might cause anguish to their parents and friends, but could not, in the absence of an ideologically-oriented ethnicity, be viewed as defection. Even so sensitive a question as intermarriage has remained, for the most part, an issue for individuals rather than for groups; romantic love conquers all, including differences in ethnic background.

We conclude, therefore, that America can tolerate the version of ethnic identification which has unfolded within it, and that the individual is not unduly constrained by the persistence of ethnicity as one form of self-location. The question that now arises is whether Negro Americans can usefully be regarded as an ethnic group.

Negroes as Ethnics

It hardly needs saying that Negroes have not been free to decide how much their Negroness shall matter. As we have already noted, racist Americans have insisted that Negroness is all-important, while liberal Americans, in the main, have insisted that Negroness is utterly irrelevant. Hence Negroes have not been parties to the general ethnic arrangement in this country. In the terms of the preceding discussion, emphasizing a kind of instrumental ethnicity, we may observe that two major groups present serious problems to that arrangement. The Jews, both ethnic group and religion, are explicitly eschatological, concerned not only with memory but also with the "Jewish future." So, too, increasingly, black Americans. For both groups, an ongoing history of discrimination has led to a kind of bet-hedging behavior: The American promise is genuinely exciting, but since it is not clear whether the promise is intended for the Jews or for the blacks, it is best to treat it skeptically. In the meantime, as the promise sporadically unfolds, it is also wise to invest some energies in the development of counter-ideologies, visions of the future which speak specifically to the problems of the especially maligned. But always quietly, lest by appearing to reject the American promise, the group in turn causes America to withdraw the promise, there being no room within its embrace for those of little faith.

It is a mark of the present despair, and growing strength, of black Americans that so many have thrown caution to the winds, and now speak out loud of a different America, with a different promise. It is a mark of the power of the American myth that still larger numbers of Negroes still accept the traditional promise, seeking only to insure that they be included in its fulfillment.

The Jews, of course, have had an easier time of it in America; free of the stigma of color, they have also been freer than Negroes to make their own decision regarding the meaning of their Jewishness. Yet it is important to note that the relatively greater freedom of Jews was available only at a price. In the American context, Jews could not be understood, and could scarcely understand themselves, as essentially an ethnic group. For if that was the category to which they belonged, how could one account for their ideological commitments, for their fierce concern with group survival? The "ethnic arrangement" is made possible when ethnic groups eschew ideology, and hence do not present themselves as competitors to, and potentially subverters of, the secular national myths. If Jews are only ethnics, they violate the arrangement.

Accordingly, both America and the Jews have been pleased, and relieved, to define the Jews as centrally a religion, one of America's great faiths. Religions enjoy some perquisites not available to ethnic groups. They are entitled, for example, to be concerned with intermarriage, with some degree of boundary maintenance, with the preservation of particularity. Jews, sensing their ethnicity, can understand the concept of an atheist Jew; for non-Jews, able to comprehend Jews only as adherents of a religious faith, the concept remains a puzzlement.

The great advantage of the Jews, in this connection, is that they have a perfectly authentic claim to religious status. But what are we to make of Negroes? Race, we have been told, is an even more incidental characteristic than ethnicity, hardly adequate qualification for admission to "the arrangement." And when race is joined by ideology, matters are made still worse. For Negroes cannot claim religious status, with the corollary exemption from limitations placed on simple ethnic groups. Insofar as Negroes are only partners in race, they lack the qualifications of ethnic groups; insofar as they are partners in ideology, they are, as it were, "over-qualified."

But race, and ethnicity, and religion, are elusive properties. The question is not whether a person is a member of one or another kind of group, but rather how certain groups in the society may most usefully be viewed. And the developing pattern of Negro behavior suggests quite powerfully that Negro Americans are best viewed as an ethnic religion, or, at the very least, an ethnic religion in-the-making.

It is not accidental that there is now a rising hostility to intermarriage among younger blacks, who, imbued with eschatological visions, conclude that intermarriage is a form of defection, hence also of betrayal. It is not accidental that some blacks, in an effort to make what is implicit in Negro communal life today explicit, have sought to establish a separate religious identity, linking themselves to Islam. Nor is it accidental that others, such as the Black Panthers, have sought to establish formal induction ceremonies that have manifestly religious qualities.

It is true, of course, that such efforts do not ring quite true; there is bound to be self-consciousness in the early stages of developing ritual, a problem older religions have long since overcome. Yet, whether current efforts gain strength, or some new and more indigenous formulation replaces them, the mere absence of formal theology should not obscure the central fact that functionally, black Americans, like Jewish Americans, are more than, hence different from, most other ethnic groups.

It is for this reason that the fitting precedent for black

community control is less the small suburban system than the parochial school. Blacks seek not only educational improvement, according to secular standards, but also the opportunity to develop an essentially private, or parochial, curriculum. The chief difficulty in such an effort is suggested quite directly by the analogy: parochial schools are not supported by the State, except indirectly. And the black community is simply incapable of developing a parochial system without direct State aid.

But the State itself is responsible both for the black need and for the black inability to meet the need. The systematic destruction of the foundations of black culture, and the persistent refusal to acknowledge the authenticity of that culture, establish the urgency of the present need; historic discrimination has prevented blacks from acquiring the resources necessary to satisfy it. Accordingly, it may well be argued that there exists a special obligation to except the Negro community from the general prohibition on State aid to parochial institutions.

In fact, by pushing the analogy to its limits, many of the objections to community control may be reduced. For if we speak not merely of a Negro school system that is similar in style to the Catholic parochial schools, but also in structure—that is, a genuinely private system managed by the community with very little auditing by the State—then it follows that the individual Negro will be offered a choice, just as Catholic students are. If, for whatever reason, he prefers the public system, which pays no particular attention to the development of black consciousness, that system is available. But if he prefers a system rooted in the community, the parochial system is at hand. Moreover, such an approach enables us, without too much discomfort, to distinguish between the black demand for community control and white "freedom of choice" plans designed to exclude blacks.

Apart from the difficulty we have in making exceptions to general principles, the main theoretical objection to a State-supported parochial school system for Negroes is that in the present climate, it is not certain that such a system would give the State its due. Would not the temptation be, instead, to deprecate white America, to mock its traditions and deride its symbols? Quite simply, if the developing black ideology is increasingly separatist, ought we expect the State to subsidize its own subversion?

While this objection cannot lightly be dismissed, there are at least two factors which blunt its edge. First, we must be reminded that we are not starting the process in an especially happy time. The question is not whether a parochial system would be less than what we hope for America, but whether it would be better than what we have, today, in America. The hostility is already with us, separatism is already here. If, as we have argued, the alienation of black Americans owes, at least in part, to the persistent refusal of even the most liberal Americans to acknowledge the authenticity of blackness, then it may be that some structural separatism might encourage greater psychological integration. It is too late to plead for faith; what is wanted is a gradual development of mutual confidence, confidence by blacks that if they accept the American future as their own, they will not be left, in the end, with nothing, confidence by white Americans that if the promise is finally made real for blacks, blacks will accept it. The events of recent years indicate quite clearly that for many Americans, separatism is not a future option, but a present reality. The question then becomes not how to avoid separatism at some future time, but how to repair it in the present—that is, how to come to grips, perhaps to terms, with those who have been neglected by the system, and feel themselves isolated from its promise. One response, quite obviously, is to accept such people on their own terms, which, in the case of black Americans, are increasingly group-oriented terms.

In short, if we are concerned with the substance of black ideology, and fearful that it may, indeed, promote ethnocentrism, we must ask whether present policies are not even more likely to have malignant consequences. What more certain way is there to insure that the Negro American group becomes a trap rather than a launching pad than to continue to insist that it is illegitimate, that the special fraternity which black Americans pursue is not authentic, that a pattern acknowledged only rarely in American social theory, but nearly everywhere in American social practice, is not applicable to black America?

Second, we may look to the history of the Catholic parochial system, which, though it began in a climate of intense suspicion, at a time when Catholics could least be expected to support the general secular culture, moved very early to a comprehensive *rapprochement* with America. Outsiders may register diverse objections to the ways in which students of the Catholic system are taught to understand America, but there can be no question that those ways are within acceptable limits. Here and there, to be sure, violations occur; generally, however, Catholic parochial education does not subvert the purposes of the State, and, in this respect, it has been getting better, rather than worse, over the years.

It may be somewhat impolitic to press the analogy to Catholic parochial schools, since many people remain bitterly opposed to the parochial model, whether because they object to what happens in parochial schools or to what fails to happen in them. Those who are persuaded that public schooling must remain the exclusive prerogative of the State, and that Negroes should not be excepted from the general rule, are bound to oppose the move towards community control. Those who recognize the continuing tension between the competing claims of the State and of the community and who acknowledge the legitimacy of Negro demands for special compensation, may take a rather different view. For them, the analogy to other institutions may be, at the least, suggestive. All the more so if it is agreed that the State's interests in education are limited rather than infinite. Beyond those interests, even though many may feel that one educational orientation is "better" than another, the choice is properly the individual's.

Thus it is not only, as some now suppose, that to acknowledge the legitimacy of Negro demands is the necessary price of social peace. There are less grudging ways of understanding those demands.

Educational Integrity

If the only source of the Negro demand for educational restructuring were the specific desire to develop group consciousness, the appropriate analogy might be to the network of afternoon or Sunday schools maintained by several other ethnic and religious groups. Those schools are specifically and exclusively about the group, and, being wholly private, are free to teach whatever they like. But, quite apart from the technical difficulties involved in establishing and maintaining such networks, the obdurate fact that the secular schools have failed to satisfy the secular needs of black students remains. A formulation is required which can address both the question of group consciousness and the problem of secular skill. Since those who insist that these two matters are closely related, that increased confidence deriving from group identity will lead to improved secular performance, may be right, and since, as we have seen, it is possible for a school to address both problems at the same time, the analogy to "add-on" systems is not especially helpful.

This brings us back to a question raised at the beginning of this chapter. Are the schools an appropriate locus for the pursuit of ethnic fraternity? The thrust of our position with respect to this question has already been presented, and can be quickly summarized: the schools are society's chief mechanism for exposing the young to organized education. The move towards public schools was an effort by the polity to assert its needs as against those of the private community, and took place at a time when the needs of the private community were relatively well-served by the general cultural environment, which was highly localized. Since that time, however, the general culture has become increasingly secular, increasingly national, and the needs of the private communities have been correspondingly neglected, except where those communities have had their own resources with which to fight against complete secularization. In consequence, the school system no longer serves to maintain a balance between the competing demands of the polity and the community.

Having for so long been accustomed to accepting the traditional understanding of the schools, it will surely be difficult to revise that understanding towards an acceptance of the role of the schools as a kind of social ballast. The schools used to be entirely Caesar's; now they are asked to render unto Caesar only a portion of their attention. Some will argue that such an effort is beyond the capability of the schools, and time may prove them right. Others will surely argue that to permit the schools to take responsibility for the private curriculum would be to threaten responsible education, professionally prescribed and professionally executed, which is the primary mission of the public schools. This, quite obviously, raises once again the question of what we mean when we speak of responsible education, a question we turn to directly. We should do well, however, to bear in mind that the source of the present crisis is precisely the inability of the public schools to provide responsible education, by any plausible definition, to significant numbers of their constituents.

This is not a treatise on educational philosophy. Yet our recognition of the responsibility of the schools to serve the needs of both the State and the community, to present both the public and the private curricula, implies as well the duty of the schools to be concerned with both affective and cognitive education. A wholly secular school system necessarily stresses the development of intellectual skills, since its challenge is to make discourse possible despite diversity. Intellectual skills are consensual, and can be defined independently of people. Affectivity is inherently more private, more volatile, less measurable, and it has the added liability of being less "teachable," in formal ways.

Proposals that educational institutions be more concerned

than they are wont to be with affective relationships are often dismissed with contempt. The plea for soft hearts is seen as coming from soft minds; schools cannot attend to love, since love is mush, and the business of the schools is disciplined inquiry. Schools must be about that which they can reward, which means that which can be measured. Insofar as the school may be permitted a concern with interpersonal relationships, that concern must be limited to a judgment of the child's capacity to cooperate with his fellows, an organizational value. They cannot judge his tendency to love his fellows, and they must, therefore, not acknowledge the need to love. Indeed, love may even be subversive, since it is blind, and, being blind, undermines the principles of performance on which the school is based.

So it is that the schools come to be about self-control, the repression of emotions with which they cannot deal formally. Silence comes to be seen as golden, leading ultimately to the *reductio ad absurdum* which Charles Silberman cites, the case of the elementary school principal who expostulates before the assembled students of his school "on the wonders of a school for the 'deaf and dumb' he had recently visited. The silence was just wonderful, he tells the assembly; the children could all get their work done because of the total silence." The goal, Silberman concludes, is explicit: "To turn normal children into youngsters behaving as though they were missing two of their faculties."[13]

There is, these days, a good deal of rather loose talk about "humanizing" education, by which, insofar as one can determine, it is often meant that education should more accurately reflect the broad scope of human concerns, and not only intellectual development. Such suggestions are frequently put forward by people who appear interested not in a balance between the affective and the cognitive, but in a romantic assertion of the primacy of the affective. Ruth Benedict, citing Nietzsche, describes the syndrome of the Dionysian:

> The Dionysian pursues (the value of existence) through 'the annihilation of the ordinary bounds and limits of

existence'; he seeks to attain in his most valued moments escape from the boundaries imposed upon him by his five senses, to break through into another order of experience. The desire of the Dionysian, in personal experience or in ritual, is to press through it toward a certain psychological state, to achieve excess. The closest analogy to the emotions he seeks is drunkenness, and he values the illumination of frenzy.[14]

Or, perhaps drugs.

But fear of the Dionysian need not lead to satisfaction with its opposite, the Apollonian, who "has often little idea of the nature of (Dionysian) experiences." It was David Riesman who observed that American culture, though often interpreted as Dionysian, is actually closer to the Apollonian model, as that model was applied by Benedict to the Pueblo Indians.[15]

The Pueblo Indians are pictured as a peaceable, cooperative society, in which no one wishes to be thought a great man and everyone wishes to be thought a good fellow. Sexual relations evoke little jealousy or other violent response; infidelity is not severely punished. Death, too, is taken in stride, with little violent emotion; in general, emotion is subdued. While there are considerable variations in economic status, there is little display of economic power and even less of political power; there is a spirit of cooperation by family and community.[16]

It is not, in short, whether you win or lose that counts, but how you play the game. And how to play the game is by the rules, which are neutral, impersonal, teachable.

The sterility of American public education, its curious lack of passion, has often drawn comment, as has its overwhelming emphasis on rules. The difficulty in reforming the atmosphere does not derive solely from the fact that many reformers appear ready, even anxious, to move to anti-intellectual extremes, but also from the fact that the schools reflect the interests of the wider culture: Louis Harris reports that two-thirds of a sample of high school students' parents believe that "maintaining discipline is more important than student self-inquiry."[17] And the difficulty also has to do with the fact that concern for affectivity speaks less to the things a teacher is supposed to do than to the very structure of the school.

Patterns of affective relationship are highly variable, and derive largely from cultural contexts. If the chief social function of the school is integrative, it follows quite naturally that the school must insist on repression, since to permit the heterogeneous patterns of affectivity to become manifest is to insure a fairly high order of disintegration. Expressive behavior is conducted in subcultural idiom; to permit such behavior is to disrupt the impersonality of cognitive endeavor. Given the tradition of public education, given the perspectives of school people, given even the mandates of an organizationally oriented society, the schools cannot acknowledge soul, or its equivalents in other subcultures.

Thus it may be that by pursuing educational integration, the school sacrifices educational integrity. Educating "the whole man," whatever that may mean, cannot proceed on the assumption that one man is, for all practical purposes, interchangeable with another—precisely the assumption that organizations, as distinguished from communities, are inclined, if not required, to make. The mistake is to suppose that the remedy for organizational excess is romantic commune, a sacrifice of all standards of performance, an exclusive reliance on secret handshakes, private passwords, and an utter disregard for whatever it is that the larger society defines as propriety.

Once again, the key word is "balance," and, because balance, also tension. The nature of that tension, and therefore of the required balance, is best explained by a set of concepts put forward by Talcott Parsons and Edward Shils.[18] Parsons and Shils propose that all human choices revolve around a set of five dichotomies. Briefly, they are:

1. Affectivity and affective neutrality, by which is meant a choice between expressing or controlling one's emotions.

2. Self-orientation and collectivity-orientation, by which

is meant a choice between acting for personal benefit and acting on behalf of collective goals. The classic illustration here is the distinction between business norms and governmental norms.

3. Universalism and particularism, by which is meant a choice between treating "the objects in a situation in accordance with a general norm covering *all* objects in that class" and treating them "in accordance with their standing in some particular relationship" to the actor. A useful illustration is the distinction between a legal system and political patronage.

4. Quality and performance, or, in an earlier version, ascription and achievement, by which is meant the choice between relating to people in terms of who they are or in terms of what they do. Quota systems are an example of the first, merit systems of the second.

5. Diffuseness and specificity, by which is meant a choice between limited obligations and open-ended obligations. Contractual obligations are specific, family roles are diffuse.

According to Parsons and Shils, these five choices exhaust all logical possibilities of orienting to social situations. Further, the choices are reflected not only in personal orientation, but in cultural propensity. In fact, social systems and cultures provide their members with substantial guidance in making their choices, because they develop characteristic biases towards one or another of the alternatives, and socialize their members accordingly.

Parsons and Shils may or may not be correct that the list is exhaustive; the important point in the present context is that the alternatives they put forward as pervasive dilemmas have developed into highly evaluative understandings. Specifically, modernity has come to be identified with universalism, affective neutrality, specificity, and performance, or achievement.[19] (The self v. collectivity choice is a bit more ambiguous.) This is not an unusual development, since the social scientific culture is no more free than other cultural systems of value biases. Accordingly, the social system comes to promote certain values, and to deprecate others. And, since societies require some degree of consistency among their components, there is a constant effort to orient individuals within the system, the value patterns of the culture, and the roles of the social system towards the same choices.

The integration is never perfect. Where it fails completely, the nation breaks apart. Where it does not fail, the several systems co-exist with more or less strain, often reducing the strain by developing *ad hoc* arrangements which permit the choices to be blurred, or which pay rhetorical homage to a set of values not generally applied in actual behavior.

The important question is what the role of the State is in connection with promoting specific value choices. The behavior of the agencies of the modern State, given social heterogeneity, must be based on those values associated with modernity. Only so can the rights of all be relatively well-protected. But that does not mean that the State must impose those same values on the social system, for the code of behavior of an institution derives, properly, from the function that institution is assigned. The State is in the business of managing conflict, and so may need one set of rules; the social system, whose function may be to provide warmth, as a kind of antidote to the necessary impersonality of government, may need a very different code. Indeed, everything we have said before suggests that the values men seek to maximize—say, in particular, both liberty and fraternity—are competing values, that the State is properly the chief defender of the first and the community of the second. It follows that to accord pre-eminence to the State, and to the code by which it is bound to operate, is to endanger the community, and the values for which men turn to it.

In an era when both parties to the continuing argument were more equally endowed—that is to say, at a time when the State was more limited and the communities more comprehensive—ceding public schooling to the State did not seem unwarranted. But today, if our argument has merit, a dangerous imbalance has developed. To redress that imbalance, communities must be ceded some authority over the schools because they appear to be the instrument best suited to the purpose.

The argument, then, is not that the schools have failed, but that they have succeeded too well, and that the values around which they have traditionally been organized now threaten other values deeply held, and not, as some have thought, pernicious. It may be too much to expect the "owner" of the schools to permit competing value systems to be introduced into them, but what may be too much to expect is not, therefore, too much to ask. In the end, the purpose is to provide the individual with options, to permit him to determine which sets of values he will choose. That is the least that liberal education can mean.

Conventional understandings of the purposes of education stress the need to prepare children for useful economic activity, to train them for civic participation, to make them able to function as members of groups, or, more properly, of organizations. But in a free society, the underlying purpose of education must go beyond these several training functions; it must be to increase personal autonomy.

Such a definition has a familiar ring. It appears to conform to Coleman's proposal that the schools be judged in terms of their success in freeing children of their social origins. But genuine freedom does not insist that those origins become irrelevant. Instead, it requires that people be provided the opportunity to make their own determination on the question of relevance. And such an opportunity, if it is to be more than a simple statement of intent, can be available only where the system provides diverse options. What is required, then, is a school system which, in its own idiom, reflects the complexity of the American arrangement, rather than one which imposes a specific version of the "right" social ordering on its participants. And that, in turn, means a school system which mirrors the tension of the arrangement. Fortunately, such flexibility is one of the luxuries a large society can afford; indeed, these days it may be a necessity, since rigid adherence to traditional patterns evokes passions that threaten the polity at its core. Moreover, failure to take advantage of the potential flexibility which size and diversity afford us is to sacrifice a major societal resource, and on a chimerical altar, to boot.

In short, community control of the schools is not a comprehensive remedy for all the ailments of public education. But it is a perfectly plausible approach to educational reform. That does not mean that community control will save us. It is no more likely to issue in salvation than any other single approach, for in a free society, no one path to salvation can satisfy. It does not even mean that community control will "succeed," however success is defined. It means only that the ideological position on which it rests is far more serious than many participants in the debate suppose.

If we are "for" community control, therefore, we are for it as a way of restoring integrity to the school system, by having the school system be about what the society is about, and not only about what the State says the society should be about. We are for it, then, as an option, since options are what a free society must be about, and, assuredly, what a free education ought to be about.

NOTES

INTRODUCTION

1. Charles V. Hamilton, "Race and Education: A Search for Legitimacy," *Harvard Education Review,* 38, No. 4 (Fall, 1968), p. 680.

CHAPTER ONE

1. The "over 50 per cent" measure is only one of several possible ways of assessing the extent of segregation. See Mary Ellen Warshauer and Robert A. Dentler, "A New Definition of School Segregation," in Robert A. Dentler, Bernard Mackler, and Mary Ellen Warshauer, eds., *The Urban R's: Race Relations as the Problem in Urban Education* (New York: Praeger, 1967), pp. 6–23.

2. This is the conclusion to be inferred from James S. Coleman *et al., Equality of Educational Opportunity,* United States Department of Health, Education, and Welfare (USGPO, 1966), commonly known as the Coleman Report, as well as from the report of the United States Commission on Civil Rights, *Racial Isolation in the Public Schools* (USGPO, 1967). The critical statement in the Coleman Report reads, "A pupil's achievement is strongly related to the backgrounds and aspirations of the other students in the school" (p. 22). This judgment is examined in some detail in the pages that follow, and especially in Chapter Three.

3. Based on case studies, Robert Crain suggests that political strategies have been substantially more successful than moral strategies. See Robert L. Crain, with the assistance of Morton Inger and others, *The Politics of School Desegregation: Comparative Case Studies of Community Structure and Policy-Making* (Chicago: Aldine, 1968).

4. See, for example, Everett F. Cataldo, Richard M. Johnson, and Lyman A. Kellstadt, "Social Strain and Urban Violence," in Louis H. Masotti and Don R. Bowen, eds., *Riots and Rebellion: Civil Violence in the Urban Community* (Beverly Hills: Sage, 1968), p. 293; *Newsweek,* June 30, 1969, p. 20; Alan A. Alt-

shuler, *Community Control: The Black Demand for Participation in Large American Cities* (New York: Pegasus, 1970), pp. 19–28.

5. From "Detroit Schools—A Blueprint for Change," by the Inner City Parents Council, reprinted in *The Liberator,* September, 1967, p. 9.

6. 269 F. Supp. 401 (1967), at 406.

7. Leonard J. Fein, "Toward the Plural City," *Technology Review,* 68, No. 8 (June, 1966), pp. 6–7.

8. Louis E. Lomax, *The Negro Revolt* (New York: Signet, 1963), pp. 202–3.

9. Lyndon Baines Johnson, *Message to Congress on Civil Rights,* January 24, 1968.

10. Norman Podhoretz, "My Negro Problem—and Ours," *Commentary,* 35 (February, 1963), pp. 93–101.

11. See, for example, the *Autobiography of Malcolm X* (New York: Grove, 1965), passim.

12. See Nathan Glazer and Daniel P. Moynihan, *Beyond the Melting Pot* (Cambridge, Mass.: M.I.T. Press, 1963).

13. Robert S. Browne, in *Separatism or Integration: Which Way for America* (New York: National Community Relations Advisory Council, 1968), p. 9.

14. Bayard Rustin, *ibid.,* p. 28.

15. See, for example, the anthology *The Black Power Revolt,* Floyd S. Barbour, ed. (Boston: Extending Horizons Books, 1968).

16. Stokley Carmichael, "Power and Racism," *New York Review of Books,* September 22, 1966.

17. Cited by Jason Epstein in "The Politics of School Decentralization," *New York Review of Books,* June 6, 1968, p. 26.

18. The Mayor's Advisory Panel on Decentralization of the New York City Schools, 1967.

19. Ibid., p. 68.

20. Ibid., p. 69.

21. Several recountings of the 1968 school crisis in New York City are available, including Naomi Levine (with Richard Cohen), *Ocean Hill-Brownsville: A Case History of Schools in Crisis* (Popular Library, 1969), and Maurice Berube and Marilyn Gittell, *Confrontation at Ocean Hill-Brownsville* (New York: Praeger, 1968).

22. Myron Lieberman, *The Future of Public Education* (Chicago: University of Chicago Press, 1960), p. 60.

23. Ibid., p. 38.

24. Mario D. Fantini, in his foreword to Marilyn Gittell, *Participants and Participation: A Study of School Policy in New York City* (New York: Praeger, 1967), p. vii.

CHAPTER TWO

1. Cicero, *Republic* (Cambridge, Mass.: Harvard University Press, 1928), I, p. 207.

2. Max Weber, "Wissenschaft als Beruf" ("Science as a Vocation"), in *Gesammelte Aufsatze zur Wissenschaftslehre,* trans. by and cited in Howard Becker and Harry Elmer Barnes, *Social Thought from Lore to Science* (New York: Dover, 1961), p. 770.

3. See, for example, Morton and Lucia White, *The Intellectual Versus the City* (Cambridge, Mass.: M.I.T. Press, 1962), and Irving Kristol, "Urban Civilization and its Discontents," *Commentary,* 50 (July, 1970), pp. 29–35.

4. Robin M. Williams, Jr., *Strangers Next Door: Ethnic Relations in American Communities* (New York: Prentice-Hall, 1964), p. 356.

5. Charles W. Anderson, Fred R. von der Mehden, and Crawford Young, *Issues of Political Development* (New York: Prentice-Hall, 1967), pp. 4–5.

6. Robert A. Nisbet, *Community and Power* (New York: Oxford University Press, 1962), p. 214.

7. Ibid., p. 22.

8. The examples are numerous, but see especially, Nisbet, *Community and Power;* Gabriel Almond and Sidney Verba, *The Civic Culture: Political Attitudes and Democracy in Five Nations, an Analytic Study* (Boston: Little, Brown, 1965); Scott Greer, *The Emerging City: Myth and Reality* (New York: Free Press, 1962); Nathan Glazer and Daniel P. Moynihan, *Beyond the Melting Pot* (Cambridge, Mass.: M.I.T. Press, 1963).

9. Tamotsu Shibutani and Kian M. Kwan, *Ethnic Stratification: A Comparative Approach* (New York: Macmillan, 1965), p. 589.

10. See the report of a Carnegie Commission on Higher Education Survey of the attitudes of American professors in the April 6, 1970, issue of the *Chronicle of Higher Education.* Liberalism is, by far, the most popular choice of the respondents.

11. Morris Janowitz, *The Community Press in an Urban Setting* (New York: Free Press, 1952); see also Scott Greer, *The Emerging City,* esp. Chap. 4, pp. 107–37.

12. National Advisory Commission on Civil Disorders (Kerner Commission), *Report* (New York: Bantam, 1968).

13. See Rashi Fein, "An Economic and Social Profile of the Negro American," in *Daedelus* (Fall, 1965), pp. 815–46.

14. This point is elaborated in Nisbet, *Community and Power,* passim.

15. "Sacred" as Howard Becker uses the term, to distinguish nonrational ties from the secular rational. See Becker, *Through*

Values to Social Interpretation; Essays on Social Contexts, Types, and Prospects (Durham, N.C.: Duke University Press, 1950).

16. Myron Lieberman, *The Future of Public Education* (Chicago: University of Chicago Press, 1960), p. 34.

17. Walter Lippmann, *The Phantom Public* (New York: Macmillan, 1925), p. 27.

18. Thomas F. Pettigrew and Patricia J. Pajonas, "Social Psychological Considerations of Racially-Balanced Schools," in *Because it is Right—Educationally,* Report of the Advisory Committee on Racial Imbalance and Education, Massachusetts Board of Education (April, 1965), pp. 97–8.

CHAPTER THREE

1. Thomas H. Eliot, "Toward an Understanding of Public School Policies," *American Political Science Review,* 52 (December, 1959), pp. 1032–52.

2. Norman D. Kerr, "The School Board as an Agency of Legitimation," *Sociology of Education,* 38 (Fall, 1964), pp. 34–59.

3. See, for example, the forthcoming studies of school boards in Chicago, Los Angeles, Boston, Columbus, and New York City, a comparative project sponsored by the Danforth Foundation.

4. Bernard R. Berelson, Paul F. Lazarsfeld, and William N. McPhee, *Voting* (Chicago: University of Chicago Press, 1954), p. 312.

5. Ibid., p. 314.

6. A more extended consideration of these issues is found in Leonard J. Fein, ed., *American Democracy: Essays on Image and Realities* (New York: Holt, Rinehart & Winston, 1964), esp. pp. 1–21, 73–77, 102–5, 131–4, 187–9, and 224–6.

7. C. Wright Mills, *The Power Elite* (New York: Oxford University Press, 1956).

8. Cremin, *The Genius of American Education* (New York: Vintage, 1965), p. 90.

9. James E. Allen, "The Public's Responsibility for Education," in Alice and Lester D. Crow, eds., *Vital Issues in American Education* (New York: Bantam, 1964), p. 89.

10. Ibid., p. 90.

11. Robert C. Wood, *Suburbia: Its People and Their Politics* (Boston: Houghton Mifflin, 1958), pp. 186–94.

12. Cited by Eliot, *Understanding Public School Policies.*

13. This also happens in smaller communities of diverse composition. See Herbert Gans, *The Levittowners* (New York: Vintage, 1969), pp. 86–103.

14. See Seymour Martin Lipset, *Political Man: The Social Bases of Politics* (Garden City: Doubleday, 1963), esp. pp. 64–70, for an extended discussion of legitimacy and effectiveness.

15. Robert A. Nisbet, *The Sociological Tradition* (New York: Basic Books, 1966), pp. 47–8.

16. Samuel Stouffer, *Communism, Conformity, and Civil Liberties* (Garden City: Doubleday, 1955), p. 130.

17. James Madison, Federalist 10, in Alexander Hamilton, John Jay, and James Madison, *The Federalist* (New York: Modern Library College Edition), p. 58.

18. See Robert A. Dahl, *A Preface to Democratic Theory* (Chicago: University of Chicago Press, 1956), esp. pp. 4–33.

19. Bundy Report, p. 17.

20. Ibid., p. 75.

21. Ibid., p. 76.

22. Ibid., p. 68.

CHAPTER FOUR

1. Plessy v. Ferguson, 163 U.S. 37 (1896).

2. Brown v. Board of Education, 347 U.S. 483 (1954).

3. Baker v. Carr, 369 U.S. 186 (1962); Gray v. Sanders, 372 U.S. 368 (1963); Wesberry v. Sanders, 376 U.S. 1 (1964); Reynolds v. Simms, 377 U.S. 533 (1963); WMCA, Inc. v. Lomenzo, 377 U.S. 633 (1964); Maryland Committee for Fair Representation v. Tawes, 377 U.S. 656 (1964); Davis v. Mann, 377 U.S. 678 (1964); Roman v. Sincock, 377 U.S. 695 (1964); Lucas v. Colorado General Assembly, 377 U.S. 713 (1964).

4. Griffin v. County School Board, 377 U.S. 218 (1964).

5. Griffin v. Illinois, 351 U.S. 12 (1956).

6. See, for example, Thomas R. Dye, "Governmental Structure, Urban Environment, and Educational Policy," *Midwest Journal of Political Science,* 11 (August, 1967), pp. 353–80. Dye finds that even when such items as property values, per capita income, and educational attainment are held constant, the number of non-whites in a school district is related to lower per pupil expenditures.

7. Samuel Bowles, "Towards Equality of Educational Opportunity," *Harvard Educational Review,* 38 (Winter, 1968), pp. 89–99.

8. The Coleman Report.

9. Frank V. Thompson, *Schooling of the Immigrant* (New York: Patterson Smith, 1920), p. 73.

10. See, especially, James S. Coleman, "Equal Schools or Equal Students," *The Public Interest,* No. 4 (Summer, 1966), pp. 70–75;

Coleman, "Towards Open Schools," *The Public Interest,* No. 9 (Fall, 1967), pp. 20–7; Coleman, "The Concept of Equal Educational Opportunity," *Harvard Educational Review,* 38 (Winter, 1968), pp. 7–22.

11. Coleman, "Equal Schools," p. 72.

12. Ibid.

13. Readers familiar with the Jensen tempest will recognize that this assumption has recently become anew a subject of considerable debate. See Arthur R. Jensen, "How Much Can We Boost IQ and Scholastic Achievement?," *Harvard Educational Review,* 39 (Winter, 1969), pp. 1–123; "Discussion" (Spring, 1969), pp. 273–356; the articles by Jensen, Richard Light and Paul Smith, Arthur Stinchcombe, and Martin Deutsch in the same journal, 39 (Summer, 1969), pp. 449–557, as well as the correspondence in that issue, pp. 581–631.

14. Thomas Pettigrew, "Race and Equal Educational Opportunity," *Harvard Educational Review,* 38 (Winter, 1968), p. 67.

15. Thomas Pettigrew and Patricia Pajonas, "Social Psychological Considerations of Racially-Balanced Schools," in *Because it is Right—Educationally: Report of the Advisory Committee on Racial Imbalance and Education* (Massachusetts State Board of Education, 1965), p. 89.

16. The Coleman Report, p. 22.

17. In United States v. School District 151 of Cook County, Illinois, 286 F. Supp. 786 (N.D. Ill., 1968).

18. Hobson v. Hansen, 269 F. Supp. 401 (D.C.D.C. 1967), at 406.

19. Robert Rosenthal and Lenore Jacobson, *Pygmalion in the Classroom* (New York: Holt, Rinehart & Winston, 1968).

20. Ibid., p. 96, 138, 145. In addition, Robert Thorndike's review of *Pygmalion* in the *American Educational Research Journal* (November, 1968), which finds serious flaws in the research.

21. See both Gerald S. Lesser, Gordon Fifer, and Donald H. Clark, "Mental Abilities of Children from Different Social-Class and Cultural Groups," *Monographs of the Society for Research in Child Development,* 30, No. 4 (1965), and Susan S. Stodolsky and Gerald Lesser, "Learning Patterns in the Disadvantaged," *Harvard Educational Review,* 5 (Fall, 1967), pp. 546–93.

22. Kenneth Clark, "Clash of Cultures in the Classroom," *Integrated Education,* 5 (August, 1963), p. 12.

23. Stodolsky and Lesser, "Learning Patterns in the Disadvantaged," pp. 582–7.

24. Ibid., pp. 584–5.

25. Ibid., pp. 585–6.

26. Ibid., p. 585.

27. John E. Coons, "Recreating the Family's Role in Education," *Inequality in Education*, Nos. 3 and 4, p. 5.

28. Berelson and Lazersfeld, *Voting*.

29. See "Interview with Leonard Covello," *The Urban Review*, 3 (January, 1969), pp. 13–19.

30. Ibid., passim.

31. See, for example, Inner City Parents Council, "Detroit Schools—A Blueprint for Change," *Liberator*, 7 (September, 1967), p. 11. The argument there presented is that a radically different curriculum should be employed in black schools. "This must not be interpreted to mean that inner city schools will not be required to meet the same grade level achievement as outlying schools. Rather, it means that this is the only method by which inner city children will be able to meet the objective achievement standards we have proposed be set by the State Board of Education."

32. The citations are from Luther W. Seabrook, "A New Experiment in Black Education," *Social Policy*, 1 (May-June, 1970), pp. 61–3. Mr. Seabrook is the principal of the new experimental Highland Park Free School in Boston.

33. Ibid., p. 61.

34. Ibid.

35. Ibid., p. 63.

36. Ibid.

37. Ibid., pp. 61–2.

CHAPTER FIVE

1. Israel Zangwill, *The Melting Pot* (New York: Macmillan, 1909), p. 37.

2. Cited in Saul K. Padover, ed., *Thomas Jefferson on Democracy* (New York: New American Library, 1946).

3. Cited by Milton Gordon, *Assimilation in American Life* (New York: Oxford University Press, 1964), p. 94.

4. Cited in Oscar Handlin, *The American People in the Twentieth Century* (Cambridge, Mass.: Harvard University Press, 1954), p. 121.

5. Gordon, *Assimilation in American Life*, pp. 84–114.

6. See, in this connection, Robert Bellah's "Civil Religion in America," in Donald R. Cutler, ed., *The Religious Situation 1968* (Boston: Beacon Press, 1968), pp. 331–55.

7. Nathan Glazer and Daniel P. Moynihan, *Beyond the Melting Pot* (Cambridge, Mass.: M.I.T. Press, 1963), p. 290.

8. Oscar Handlin, "Historical Perspectives on the American Ethnic Group," *Daedalus* (Spring, 1961), p. 232.

9. Horace M. Kallen, *Culture and Democracy in the United States* (New York: Boni and Liveright, 1924).

10. Henry Jackson Turner, *The Frontier in American History* (New York: Henry Holt, 1920), p. 190.

11. See Gordon, *Assimilation in American Life,* esp. pp. 60–83.

12. Cited in Oscar Handlin, *Boston's Immigrants* (New York: Atheneum, 1968), p. 135.

13. Charles Silberman, "Murder in the Schoolroom," *The Atlantic,* 225, No. 6 (June, 1970), p. 86.

14. Ruth Benedict, *Patterns of Culture* (New York: Mentor, 1946), p. 79.

15. David Riesman, *The Lonely Crowd* (New Haven: Yale University Press, 1961), pp. 225–35.

16. Ibid., p. 226.

17. Cited by Silberman, "Murder in the Schoolroom," p. 92.

18. In *Toward a General Theory of Action* (Cambridge, Mass.: Harvard University Press, 1951).

19. For one example, see F. X. Sutton, "Social Theory and Comparative Politics," in Harry Eckstein and David E. Apter, eds., *Comparative Politics* (New York: Free Press, 1963), pp. 67–81.

INDEX